First World War
and Army of Occupation
War Diary
France, Belgium and Germany

37 DIVISION
112 Infantry Brigade
East Lancashire Regiment
8th Battalion
30 July 1915 - 21 February 1918

WO95/2537/4

The Naval & Military Press Ltd
www.nmarchive.com
Published in association with The National Archives

Published by

The Naval & Military Press Ltd

Unit 10 Ridgewood Industrial Park,

Uckfield, East Sussex,

TN22 5QE England

Tel: +44 (0) 1825 749494

www.naval-military-press.com

www.nmarchive.com

This diary has been reprinted in facsimile from the original. Any imperfections are inevitably reproduced and the quality may fall short of modern type and cartographic standards.

© **Crown Copyright**
Images reproduced by permission of The National Archives, London, England, 2015.

Contents

Document type	Place/Title	Date From	Date To
Heading	WO95/2537/4		
Heading	37th Division 112th Infy Bde 8th Bn East Lancs Regt Aug 1915-Feb 1918		
Heading	112th Inf. Bde. 37th Div. Battn. disembarked Boulogne from England 1.8.15 8th Battn. The East Lancashire Regiment. August 30.7.15 to 31.8 15 1915		
War Diary	Ludgershall	30/07/1915	31/07/1915
War Diary	Nielle Lez Ardres	02/08/1915	02/08/1915
War Diary	Arques	04/08/1915	04/08/1915
War Diary	Hazebrouck	05/08/1915	15/08/1915
War Diary	Dranoutre	17/08/1915	22/08/1915
War Diary	Godewaersvelde	24/08/1915	24/08/1915
War Diary	Amplier	25/08/1915	25/08/1915
War Diary	Mailly	28/08/1915	31/08/1915
Heading	112th Inf. Bde. 37th Div. 8th Battn. The East Lancashire Regiment. September 1915		
War Diary	Mailly	01/09/1915	02/09/1915
War Diary	St Amand	05/09/1915	13/09/1915
War Diary	Fonquevillers	16/09/1915	28/09/1915
War Diary	St Amand	30/09/1915	30/09/1915
Heading	112th Inf. Bde. 37th Div. 8th Battn. The East Lancashire Regiment October 1915		
Miscellaneous	To D.A.G. Base	02/11/1915	02/11/1915
War Diary	St Amand	02/10/1915	08/10/1915
War Diary	Fonquevillers	10/10/1915	20/10/1915
War Diary	Souastre	22/10/1915	31/10/1915
Heading	112th Inf. Bde. 37th Div. 8th Battn. The East Lancashire Regiment. November 1915		
War Diary	Foncquevillers	02/11/1915	30/11/1915
Heading	112th Inf. Bde. 37th Div. 8th Battn. The East Lancashire Regiment. December 1915		
War Diary	Foncquevillers	02/12/1915	08/12/1915
War Diary	Souastre	10/12/1915	19/12/1915
War Diary	Foncquevillers	20/12/1915	31/12/1915
Heading	112th Brigade. 37th Division. 1/8th Battalion East Lancashire Regiment January 1916		
War Diary	Foncquevillers	01/01/1916	01/01/1916
War Diary	Souastre	02/01/1916	13/01/1916
War Diary	Foncquevillers	14/01/1916	25/01/1916
War Diary	Souastre	26/01/1916	31/01/1916
Heading	112th Brigade 37th Division 1/8th Battalion East Lancashire Regiment February 1916		
Miscellaneous	Memorandum		
Heading	37 8th E Lancs Vol 7 Feb 1916		
War Diary	Souastre	01/02/1916	04/02/1916
War Diary	Foncquevillers	07/02/1916	13/02/1916
War Diary	Humbercamps	15/02/1916	16/02/1916
War Diary	Berles	19/02/1916	22/02/1916
War Diary	Humbercamps	23/02/1916	29/02/1916

Heading	112th Brigade 37th Division. 1/8th Battalion East Lancashire Regiment March 1916		
War Diary	Humbercamps	01/03/1916	08/03/1916
War Diary	Foncquevillers	09/03/1916	12/03/1916
War Diary	Pommier	14/03/1916	27/03/1916
Heading	112th Brigade. 37th Division. 1/8th Battalion East Lancashire Regiment April 1916		
Miscellaneous	To. Oc/c A.G. Office	29/05/1916	29/05/1916
War Diary	St Amand	01/04/1916	17/04/1916
War Diary	Sus St Leger	18/04/1916	30/04/1916
Heading	112th Brigade 37th Division 1/8th Battalion East Lancashire Regiment May 1916		
Miscellaneous	To O/C A.G.S. Office		
Miscellaneous	Memorandum		
War Diary	Sooastre	02/05/1916	02/05/1916
War Diary	Foncquevillers	03/05/1916	10/05/1916
War Diary	Hannescamps	11/05/1916	14/05/1916
War Diary	Bavincourt	16/05/1916	16/05/1916
War Diary	Hannescamps	26/05/1916	31/05/1916
Heading	112th Brigade. 37th Division. Battalion went to 34th Division 5th July 1916. Rejoined 37th Division 21st August 1916 1/8th Battalion East Lancashire Regiment June 1916		
War Diary	Hannescamp	01/06/1916	06/06/1916
War Diary	Bavincourt	07/06/1916	11/06/1916
War Diary	Bienvillers	16/06/1916	17/06/1916
War Diary	Bavincourt	18/06/1916	18/06/1916
War Diary	Hannescamps	19/06/1916	30/06/1916
Heading	112th Brigade. 37th Division. 34th Division from 5.7.16 Transferred with 112th Brigade from 37th Division to 34th Division 5.7.16 8th Battalion East Lancashire Regiment July 1916		
War Diary	Hannescamps	01/07/1916	03/07/1916
War Diary	Pommier	03/07/1916	03/07/1916
War Diary	Halloy	04/07/1916	05/07/1916
War Diary	Millencourt	06/07/1916	06/07/1916
War Diary	Becourt Wood	06/07/1916	07/07/1916
War Diary	Heligoland	08/07/1916	10/07/1916
War Diary	Close Support	11/07/1916	14/07/1916
War Diary	Pozieres	15/07/1916	15/07/1916
War Diary	Close Support	16/07/1916	16/07/1916
War Diary	Albert	17/07/1916	17/07/1916
War Diary	Bresle	18/07/1916	19/07/1916
War Diary	Behencourt	21/07/1916	31/07/1916
Heading	112th Brigade. 34th Division till 21st August. Rejoined 37th Division. 21st August 1916. Battalion Rejoined 37th Division 21.8.16 1/8th Battalion East Lancashire Regiment August 1916		
Heading	War Diary of 8th (S) Bn. East Lancashire Regt. from 1.8.16 to 31.8.16 Volume 13		
War Diary	Becourt Wood	01/08/1916	29/08/1916
Heading	112th Brigade. 37th Division. 1/8th Battalion East Lancashire Regiment September 1916		
Miscellaneous	To Headquarters 112 Infantry Brigade Confidential war Diary of 8th (5) Bn East Lancashire Regt. from 1-9-16 to 30-9-16 Volume 14		

War Diary		01/09/1916	02/09/1916
War Diary	Dieval	05/09/1916	18/09/1916
War Diary	Fosse	19/09/1916	20/09/1916
War Diary	Angres II	21/09/1916	26/09/1916
Heading	112th Brigade 37th Division. 1/8th Battalion East Lancashire Regiment October 1916		
Heading	War Diary of 8th S Bn. East Lancashire Regt. from 1-10-16 to 31-10-16 Volume 15		
War Diary	Fosse 10	01/10/1916	02/10/1916
War Diary	Angres II	03/10/1916	04/10/1916
War Diary	Angres I	04/10/1916	07/10/1916
War Diary	Angres II	13/10/1916	15/10/1916
War Diary	Coupigny	16/10/1916	16/10/1916
War Diary	Beugin	18/10/1916	18/10/1916
War Diary	Averdoingt	20/10/1916	20/10/1916
War Diary	Sibiville	21/10/1916	21/10/1916
War Diary	Hem	22/10/1916	22/10/1916
War Diary	Sarton	23/10/1916	23/10/1916
War Diary	Bertrancourt	25/10/1916	25/10/1916
War Diary	Marieux	30/10/1916	30/10/1916
Heading	112th Brigade. 37th Division. 1/8th Battalion East Lancashire Regiment November 1916		
Heading	War Diary of 8th East Lancashire Regt. Volume 16		
War Diary	Doullens	01/11/1916	15/11/1916
War Diary	North of Ancre	15/11/1916	30/11/1916
Heading	112th Brigade. 37th Division. 1/8th Battalion East Lancashire Regiment December 1916		
Heading	To Headqtr 112 Infy Bde. War Diary of 8th S. Bn East Lancashire Regt from 1-12-16 to 31-12-16 Volume 17		
War Diary	Val de Maison	03/12/1916	20/12/1916
War Diary	Robecq	21/12/1916	28/12/1916
Heading	War Diary 8th East Lancs January 1917 Vol 18		
Heading	To Headqtr 112 Infantry Brigade War Diary of 8th Bn East Lancashire Regt. From 1-1-17 to 31-1-17 Volume 18	31/01/1917	31/01/1917
War Diary	Festubert Left Sub Section	03/01/1917	08/01/1917
War Diary	Le Touret	09/01/1917	10/01/1917
War Diary	Festubert Left Sub Section	05/01/1917	05/01/1917
War Diary	Le Touret	21/01/1917	29/01/1917
Heading	To Headqtr 112 Infy Bde War Diary of 8th S. Bn. East Lancashire Regt. From 1-2-17 to 28-2-17 Volume 19		
War Diary	Locon	04/02/1917	10/02/1917
War Diary	Loos (Right)	11/02/1917	16/02/1917
War Diary	Loos Right	07/02/1917	26/02/1917
Heading	To Headqtr 112 Infy Bde War Diary of 8th Bn East Lancashire Regt. 1-3-17 to 31-3-17 Volume 20		
War Diary	Maroc	02/03/1917	02/03/1917
War Diary	Rebruviette	09/03/1917	09/03/1917
Heading	To Headqtrs 112 Infy Bde. Confidential War Diary of 8th Bn. East Lancashire Regt. Volume 21 1-4-17 to 30-4-17 Vol 21		
War Diary	Rebruviette	04/04/1917	04/04/1917
War Diary	Lattre St Quentin	05/04/1917	05/04/1917
War Diary	Wanquentin	08/04/1917	30/04/1917

Heading	To Headqtr 112 Infy Bde. Confidential War Diary of 8th Bn East Lancashire Regt. Volume 22 From 1-5-17 to 1-6-17 Vol 22		
War Diary	Ambrines	01/05/1917	25/05/1917
War Diary	Wancourt	26/05/1917	01/06/1917
Heading	War Diary 8th East Lancs June 1917 Vol 23		
Heading	To Headqtr 112 Infy Bde Confidential War Diary of 8th Bn East Lancashire Regt From 1-6-17 to 30-6-17 Volume 23		
War Diary	Duisans	02/06/1917	02/06/1917
War Diary	Izel Lez Hameau	03/06/1917	06/06/1917
War Diary	Valhoun & Le Hamel	07/06/1917	07/06/1917
War Diary	Dennebroecq	07/06/1917	22/06/1917
War Diary	Neuffpre & Picquer	23/06/1917	23/06/1917
War Diary	St Sylvestre Capel	24/06/1917	24/06/1917
War Diary	Locre	25/06/1917	28/06/1917
War Diary	N 23 a. 7.7	29/06/1917	30/06/1917
Heading	To Headqtr 112 Infy Bde. Confidential War Diary of 8th Bn East Lancashire Regt. From July 1st to July 30		
War Diary	Dranoutre	01/07/1917	10/07/1917
War Diary	Kemmel	11/07/1917	18/07/1917
War Diary	Kemmel & Trenches	19/07/1917	22/07/1917
War Diary	Trenches	23/07/1917	25/07/1917
War Diary	Trenches & Lancashire Village	26/07/1917	26/07/1917
War Diary	Lancashire Village & Dranoutre	26/07/1917	26/07/1917
War Diary	Dranoutre	27/07/1917	30/07/1917
Heading	War Diary 8th East Lancs Aug 1917		
War Diary		30/07/1917	03/08/1917
War Diary	Wakefield Huts	02/08/1917	04/08/1917
War Diary	Swindon Camp	04/08/1917	31/08/1917
Heading	To Headqtr 112 Infy Bde Confidential War Diary of 8th Bn East Lancashire Regt. Volume 26 from 1-9-17 to 30-9-17 Vol 26		
War Diary	Siege Farm	01/09/1917	30/09/1917
Heading	War Diary of 8th (Service) Battalion East Lancashire Regiment from 1st October 1917 to 31st October 1917 Volume 26 Vol 27		
War Diary		01/10/1917	08/10/1917
War Diary	Cants	08/10/1917	17/10/1917
War Diary	Inkerman Camp	18/10/1917	30/11/1917
Heading	To Headqtr 112 Infy Bde Confidential War Diary of 8th (S) Bn East Lancashire Regt. Volume 28 From 1-12-17 to 31-12-17		
War Diary	Dezon Camp	01/12/1917	14/12/1917
War Diary	Ridge Wood	15/12/1917	21/12/1917
War Diary	De Zon	22/12/1917	29/12/1917
War Diary	Line	29/12/1917	17/01/1918
War Diary	La Bell Hotesse	18/01/1918	21/01/1918
War Diary	Dickebusch	22/01/1918	31/01/1918
Heading	To A.G. Confidential War Diary of 8th Bn East Lancashire Rgt From 1-2-18 to 22-2-18 Volume 31		
War Diary	Dickebusch	01/02/1918	04/02/1918
War Diary	Bandringhem	05/02/1918	20/02/1918
War Diary	Berthen	21/02/1918	21/02/1918

Woods 2/5/37 4/14

37TH DIVISION
112TH INFY BDE

8TH BN EAST LANCS REGT
AUG 1915 - FEB 1918

DISBANDED

112th Inf.Bde.
37th Div.

Battn. disembarked
Boulogne from
England 1.8.15.

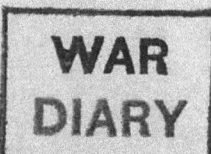

8th BATTN. THE EAST LANCASHIRE REGIMENT.

A U G U S T

(30.7.15 to 31.8.15)

1 9 1 5

Feb 18

WAR DIARY
or
INTELLIGENCE SUMMARY.
(Erase heading not required.)

Army Form C. 2118.

Instructions regarding War Diaries and Intelligence Summaries are contained in F.S. Regs., Part II. and the Staff Manual respectively. Title pages will be prepared in manuscript.

Place	Date	Hour	Summary of Events and Information	Remarks and references to Appendices
LUDGERSHALL	30.7.15		Advance Party consisting of 4 Officers (2nd in Command, Transport, Machine Gun, & Chaplain (R.C.)) & 102 other ranks left LUDGERSHALL station at 3.0 A.M. for SOUTHAMPTON en route for HAVRE, with all transport and vehicles. (A.B.C.& D Coys)	9pm O.R. 4 102
LUDGERSHALL	31.7.15		The remainder of the Battalion left LUDGERSHALL station by two trains at 4.40 p.m. and 5.15 p.m. respectively, en route for BOULOGNE arriving there at 12.15 A.M. on August 1st.	1st Train 15 372 2nd " 12 380
P.H.			The Battalion on arrival marched to OSTREHOVE Camp and encamped under canvas for the night.	27 752
NIELLE LEZ ARDRES	2.8.15		The Battalion left OSTREHOVE Camp at 10.30 p.m. for PONT DE BRIQUES station, where it entrained. The Advance Party was in the train having come from HAVRE also at the Regimental Transport. The complete Battalion detrained at AUDRUICK at 4.0 A.M. and proceeded to NIELLE LEZ ARDRES, where billets were found where taken up.	
P.H.				
ARQUES	4.8.15		The Battalion left NIELLE LEZ ARDRES at 7.30 A.M. for NORDAUSQUES when it joined the rest of the 112th 1st Brigade en route for ARQUES via TILQUE and going round S.t OMER on the S. side. Billets were taken up in ARQUES for the night. During the march a halt was made from 12.0 till 2.0 A.M. The sleep was bad and many men fell out.	
P.H.				

INTELLIGENCE SUMMARY.

(Erase heading not required.)

Place	Date	Hour	Summary of Events and Information	Remarks and references to Appendices
HAZEBROUCK P.H.	5.8.15		The Battalion left ARQUES at 7.0 A.M. en route with the 112th Brigade for HAZEBROUCK. There was a halt at midday from 12.0 – 1.30 p.m. The day was warm and over fell out frequently. On arrival at HAZEBROUCK the Battalion was billeted in the Hospital (not completely built) in the Avenue de HONDEGHEM, together with the 11th R. Warwick Regt.	
HAZEBROUCK P.H.	8.8.15		On Sunday, 8th inst. the Battalion together with the 11th R. Warwick Regt., was inspected by General PLUMER, G.O.C. 2nd Army Corps, at 10.45 A.M.	
HAZEBROUCK	10.8.15		A detachment of 581 N.C.Os and men with the necessary transport and 19 officers went to LOCRE to dig trenches. Major Magrath was in charge. This Detachment joined the rest of the Brigade at 7.0 A.M. Major Webster (10th L.N. Lanc.) took charge of the Brigade detachment. The Machine Gun Section, Signallers & Band remained in HAZEBROUCK.	Apex O.R. 19. 381
HAZEBROUCK P.H.	15.8.15		No. 18662 Pte. Bradney found drowned near MERVILLE in canal. Buried by 10th Worcester Regt.	
DRANOUTRE	17.8.15		C.O. and Adjutant left HAZEBROUCK for DRANOUTRE. Col Melvill took charge of 2nd half Bn. whilst at the latter place. No. 17608 Pte. Dodson was wounded in leg by rifle bullet this evening about 9.30 p.m. when on the road near Grazing Station near R.E. FARM.	
DRANOUTRE P.H.	20.8.15	9.30 p.m	No. 17647 Pte. Bristow & No. 17192 Pte. Spitt were wounded in held by ricochet'g on road near R.E. Farm.	

INTELLIGENCE SUMMARY.

(Erase heading not required.)

Place	Date	Hour	Summary of Events and Information	Remarks and references to Appendices
DRANOUTRE	22.8.15	5.10 p.m.	No 16627 Sergt Parker slightly wounded on knee (returned to duty) by a shell splinter. Four shells (about 8") burst over the camp occupied by E Coys & 11th R Warwicks. By orders of the Major Gen (Count Gleichen) the camp was changed to the West of DRANOUTRE. This was accomplished by 9.30 p.m. These shells were evidently intended for an aerowork balloon, about 1000 yards to the West of the camp, and not for the camp itself.	
P.H.	24.8.15		The 11th Inf Bde Detachment left DRANOUTRE at 1.0 p.m. to proceed to GODEWAERSVELDE, arriving there at 6.0 p.m.. The remainder of the Battalion marched from HAZEBROUCK the same day (24.8.15)	
GODEWAERSVELDE				
P.H.			The complete Battalion was billeted for the night in barns near GODEWAERSVELDE, arriving at 9.33 p.m.	
AMPLIER	26.8.15		The complete Battalion left GODEWAERSVELDE station in one train for DOULLENS, arriving there at 4.10 A.M. on 26.8.15. The Battalion then marched to AMPLIER, a village about 5 miles EAST of DOULLENS and was billeted in Barns and bivouacs.	
P.H.				
MAILLY.	28.8.15		The Battalion left AMPLIER at 8.30 A.M. on 27.8.15 & marched to MAILLY. A halt was made at ACHEUX from 12.45 to 3.0 p.m. for dinners and taking in supplies. MAILLY was reached at 5.30 p.m. The march between ACHEUX and MAILLY was done by Companies (one at a time) with ten (10) minutes interval between each. The Battalion went into billets at MAILLY. As this town was only a mile from the	

INTELLIGENCE SUMMARY.

(Erase heading not required.)

Place	Date	Hour	Summary of Events and Information	Remarks and references to Appendices
MAILLY B.H.	28.8.15		firing line, whilst trenches were dug by Companies for all men who could not be accommodated in cellars. The Battalion was attached to the 12th Inf. Bde. for instruction.	
MAILLY B.H.	31.8.15		The Battalion less Transport, Band, and a few Regimentally employed went into the trenches on the evening of the 29.8.15. at 7.30 p.m. i.e. left MAILLY at that time. The Coys were distributed in the 12th Inf. Bde as follows:— "A" Coy. to Essex Regt. "B" Coy. to Kings Own Regt. "C" to LANCS. FUS. "D" to S. LANCS Regt. The Battn. H.Q. staff did not go, but waited the Trenches at day time on the 30th & today.	Given O.R. 20./774 in Trenches.

112th Inf.Bde.
37th Div.

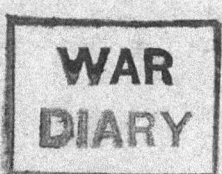

8th BATTN. THE EAST LANCASHIRE REGIMENT.

S E P T E M B E R

1 9 1 5

Army Form C. 2118.

S.E. Lawes

INTELLIGENCE SUMMARY.
(Erase heading not required.)

Place	Date	Hour	Summary of Events and Information	Remarks and references to Appendices
MAILLY	1.9.15		Casualties on 31.8.15:— Killed:- No.16583 Pte. Vanden. H. Wounded:- No. 16166 Pte. Hanvey. J. (Head) No.14942. Pte. Hargreaves. R. (calf) No. 16457 Pte. Robinson. S. (slight) 16256 L.Cpl. Darlington. H. No. 16632 Pte. Sixsmith. W.	16583 Killed. Officer O.R. Nil. 2
			Casualties on 1.9.15.:— Killed:— No.16180 Pte. Pearse. G. Wounded:— No.16432 Pte. Hampson. W. No.6760 C.Sgt. M. Sidgreaves No. 16176 Pte. Morgan. L. No. 16628 Pte. Andrews. W. No.14951 Sgt. Skelly. N. No. 16164 Pte. Pollard. R. No.17101 Pte. Williams. W.	Wounded Officer O.R. Nil. 12
			All the above Casualties occurred in the Trenches, while the Battn. was undergoing instruction with the 12th Inf. Bde. at MAILLY, and were due to Shrapnel, Grenades & Aerial Torpedoes.	
MAILLY.	2.9.15		No.16256 L.Cpl. Darlington. H. died, buried in local Cemetry, Beauval. The Companies left their Trenches together with the Battn. to which they were attached	
ST AMAND	6.9.15		The Battalion left MAILLY for ST AMAND assembling at BERTRANCOURT at 10.0 a.m. & arriving at ST AMAND at 3.15 p.m. when billets were taken up. 5.9.15.	
ST AMAND	9.9.15		The Battn. less M.G. Section Men to be trained in Bomb Throwing etc. Stretcher Bearers (Band) & signallers left for BIENVILLERS to dig trenches by night. The digging was done under supervision of the R.E. Cup started to dig at 9.30 p.m. 9.9.15.	

8th E. Lancs

INTELLIGENCE SUMMARY
(Erase heading not required.)

Summary of Events and Information

Place	Date	Hour	Summary of Events and Information	Remarks and references to Appendices
ST AMAND	13.9.15		The Digging Party returned from BIENVILLERS on the 12.9.15. On 13.9.15 2 Officers, 8 N.C.Os. & 7 Men went into the Trenches of the 10th R. Fusiliers for instruction prior to taking over on the 16th.9.15.	
FONQUEVILLERS	16.9.15		The relief of the 10th R. Fusiliers was completed by 10.40 p.m. on the 15.9.15. The Q.M., Transport Officers and Coy. Q.M. Sergts remained with the Transport in ST AMAND. The 10th R. Fusiliers took over the billets occupied by the Battn. in ST AMAND. The Battn. left ST AMAND by Companies; B Coy & A Coy left at 5.30 p.m. & 5.40 p.m. respectively, C and D Coys at 6.0 p.m. The route was by metalled road to FONQUEVILLERS. At the Western end of FONQUEVILLERS, guides from the 10th R. Fusiliers met the Coys. to guide them to their positions, viz:– A & B in the fire trenches, C & D in Reserve; B Coy on right A Coy on Left. The 10th L.N. Lancs Regt. were on the Left of the Battn. & the 1/8th R. Warwick. Regt. on the right; this latter belonged to the 48th Division. The night was very dark. No patrols were sent out and no men were allowed to sleep.	

Instructions regarding War Diaries and Intelligence Summaries are contained in F.S. Regs., Part II. and the Staff Manual respectively. Title pages will be prepared in manuscript.

INTELLIGENCE SUMMARY.
8th E. Lancs.
(Erase heading not required.)

Place	Date	Hour	Summary of Events and Information	Remarks and references to Appendices
FONQUEVILLERS	17.9.15	9.30AM	The situation has been normal for the past 24 hrs. Patrols were sent out last night but had nothing to report on return. A few shells (4 in number) fell near Battn. Head Quarters at 3.0 p.m. on the 16.9.15.; one of these fell on one of the buildings about 10 yards from H.Q. No. 20640 Corpl. McMULLAN A. was hit in the thigh by an accidental discharge of a rifle in his section at 5:30 a.m. 2/Lt HUMPHREYS left en route for WISQUES for a course of Mach. Guns.	Casualties Officer O.R. Nil 1.
FONQUEVILLERS	18.9.15	9.30 AM	The situation has been normal. Working parties were employed improving the parapets and mending the wire entanglements. No. 17302 Pte CHARNLEY E. was hit by a bullet at about 10.0 p.m. injuring his arm, testicles & thigh.	Casualties Officer O.R. Nil 1
FONQUEVILLERS	19.9.15	9.30 am	The situation has been quiet for the past 24 hrs. Fatigue parties of 100 O.R. in all, were supplied to the R.E. on the 16th 17th 18th insts.	
FONQUEVILLERS	20.9.15	9.30 a.m.	The situation has been normal. Last night at 5.0 p.m. order (verbal) were received from 112th Bde H.Q. that passages were to be cut (353–353) in the wire covering our front in case it might be necessary to advance.	

Instructions regarding War Diaries and Intelligence Summaries are contained in F.S. Regs., Part II. and the Staff Manual respectively. Title pages will be prepared in manuscript.

INTELLIGENCE SUMMARY — 8th E. Lanes.
(Erase heading not required.)

Place	Date	Hour	Summary of Events and Information	Remarks and references to Appendices
FONQUEVILLERS	21.9.15		No 14073 Sergt. DAVIDSON was killed in the S. FORTIN by two bullets one in throat one in breast. No 16110 Pte. KNOWLES was wounded in stomach at the same place, serious. Orders were given for wire cutting operations to be continued C. & D. Coys relieved A & B Coys in the trenches. Relief started at 5.30 p.m. finished 7.15 p.m.	Casualties Officer / O.R. Nil / 2
FONQUEVILLERS	22.9.15		Orders were received from H.Q. 112 Inf. Bde that the R.F.A. were going to bombard the enemys front trenches and that men should have cover over rear at hand in case of retaliation by the enemy. The enemy did not retaliate.	
"	23.9.15		Last night orders came from H.Q. 112 Inf. Bde that R.F.A were going to cut the enemys wire at 10. A.M today. The bombardment started at 11.0 A.M. and finished at dusk. The wire was cut in 6 places in front of our sector. No 14987 Pte AUSTIN J. was shot dead in the S. FORTIN. (Comdg at FONQUEVILLERS	Casualties Officer O.R. Nil / 1
"	24			
"	24.9.15		The R.F.A continued to bombard the enemy's wire and trenches. The gaps made were kept open as much as possible by Mach. Gun & rifle fire. The enemy however managed to repair their damage slightly.	

INTELLIGENCE SUMMARY. 8th — E. Lancs

(Erase heading not required.)

Place	Date	Hour	Summary of Events and Information	Remarks and references to Appendices
FONQUEVILLERS	26.9.15		Nothing unusual happened. The R.F.A. fired a few shells at the enemy's am and trenches, but only about 5 rounds per gun.	
"	28.9.15		The Battalion was relieved by the 10th Battn. R. Fusiliers. The relief started at 6.30 p.m and was completed by 9.15 p.m. The Battn then marched to HUMBERCAMP via SOUASTRE to camp under canvas, arriving there at 1:15. A.M.	
ST AMAND	30.9.15		The Battalion moved to ST AMAND on 29.9.15. to billets in barns. Two companies were given baths at PAS in morning of 29.9.15. The remaining Coys had baths today. Weather cold and wet.	

112th Inf.Bde.
37th Div.

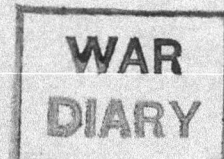

8th BATTN. THE EAST LANCASHIRE REGIMENT.

O C T O B E R

1 9 1 5

To:- D.A.G.
   Base.

                    2-11-15.

Herewith War diary of
8th Battn. E. Lancs. Regt.

           P. Hammond
              Capt
           Adjt. 8. E. Lancs.

INTELLIGENCE SUMMARY.

8th East Lancs

(Erase heading not required.)

Place	Date	Hour	Summary of Events and Information	Remarks and references to Appendices
ST AMAND	2.10.15		Lt Col. MACKAY of the 1st Hauts Regt arrived to take over command of the Battalion from Col. J.S. MELVILLE. He took command from 1. Oct 1915.	
ST AMAND	4.10.15		A draft of 50 men arrived for the Battn. They entrained at AUTHIEULE 4.10.15.	
ST AMAND	8.10.15		A draft of 19 men arrived for the Battn. on 8.10.15.	
FONQUEVILLERS	10.10.15		The Battn. relieved the 10th R. Fus. Regt in the trenches. Relief started at 5.40 p.m. & was completed at 7.54 p.m.	
"	13.10.15		At about 7.0 p.m. the enemy opened heavy rifle & m. gun fire on our trenches and the village. His artillery dropped about 50 shells into our firing and support Trenches. This bombardment lasted about ¾ hr. Casualties Pte Stanus & Sergt Edwards on 13.10.15. L/Cpl Watson & Pte Kellett, wounded 12.10.15. Pte Kellett slightly at duty, Stanus slightly at duty. L/Cpl Dennis wounded on 13.10.15.	

8 — E. Lewis

INTELLIGENCE SUMMARY.
(Erase heading not required.)

Place	Date	Hour	Summary of Events and Information	Remarks and references to Appendices
FONQUEVILLERS	18.10.15		Pte Shields wounded on 15.10.15. A & B Coys were relieved by C & D Coys.	
"	19.10.15		No 10744 L/Cpl Wilson wounded 18.10.15.	
"	20.10.15		No 17714 Pte Barlow wounded 19.10.15	
SOUASTRE	22.10.15		The Battalion was relieved in the trenches by the 10th R. Fusiliers. The relief started at 5.30 & was completed at 7.30 p.m. The Battn marched to billets to SOUASTRE.	
"	26.10.15		The Battn furnished a guard of honour for H.M. The King, The Pres. of France at MARIEUX. The guard consisted of 100 rank & file and 3 officers Capt. Collymore being in command. This guard was complimented on their smartness.	
"	31.10.15		No 16307 Pte Sergeant J. wounded at No 6 Post 20. Pte Lee J. were casualties on 29.10.15. Those men had been attached to a Tunnelling Coy.	

112th Inf.Bde.
37th Div.

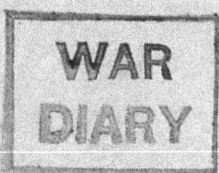

8th BATTN. THE EAST LANCASHIRE REGIMENT.

N O V E M B E R

1 9 1 5

INTELLIGENCE SUMMARY.

(Erase heading not required.)

Place	Date	Hour	Summary of Events and Information	Remarks and references to Appendices
FONCQUEVILLERS	3-11-15		The Battn relieved the 10th Bn R. Fus Regt in the trenches. Relief was started 4·0 pm and completed 6·30 pm.	
	4-11-15		18444 Pte J. Kennedy was wounded in Stomach 4-11-15 died of Wounds 5-11-15 — 19 C.C.S. DOULLENS.	
	5-11-15		17782 Pte Summerfield was wounded Rifle Wound back of R. Shoulder.	
	9-11-15		17753 Pte E. Grines Wounded Left Shoulder.	
	10-11-15		The Enemy Bombarded our position with Aerial Torpedos and High Explosive. The weather was very wet and trenches were in awful state.	
	10-11-15		Lieut J. W. Parkes was transferred to this Battn from 1st Battn & assumed duties of Adjutant 11-11-15.	

INTELLIGENCE SUMMARY.

(Erase heading not required.)

Summaries regarding War Diaries and Intelligence Summaries are contained in F. S. Regs., Part II. and the Staff Manual respectively. Title pages will be prepared in manuscript.

Place	Date	Hour	Summary of Events and Information	Remarks and references to Appendices
FONCQUEVILLERS.	10.11.15		1956 Pte Wostall and 1949 Pte Stewart were wounded by fall of trenches after bombardment with Aerial Torpedo.	
	11.11.15		22545 Pte Barnes was wounded by Aerial Torpedo. 17269 Pte Thoburn was wounded by H.E. Shell in Left Shoulder.	
	14.11.15		The Battalion was relieved by 10th R Fus. The relief started at 3.30 pm and was complete 5.45 pm.	
	16.11.15		The Battalion was allotted the Baths at PAS.	
	18.11.15		Fatigues of 500 men were furnished for work on Trenches at BIENVILLERS and FONCQUEVILLERS. These fatigues were found alternate days with 11th Bn Royal Warwicks.	

INTELLIGENCE SUMMARY.

(Erase heading not required.)

Summaries are contained in F.S. Regs., Part II. and the Staff Manual respectively. Title pages will be prepared in manuscript.

Place	Date	Hour	Summary of Events and Information	Remarks and references to Appendices
FONCAVILLERABLE			The Battalion relieved the 10th Bn R Fus relief was started at 3.0pm and completed 5.30pm.	
	30-1-15		The situation has been very quiet although the weather was very wet and the Trenches are in a very dilapidated state and almost impassable.	

112th Inf.Bde.
37th Div.

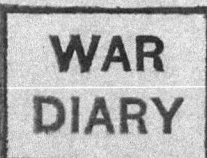

8th BATTN. THE EAST LANCASHIRE REGIMENT.

D E C E M B E R

1 9 1 5

INTELLIGENCE SUMMARY

Place	Date	Hour	Summary of Events and Information	Remarks and references to Appendices
FONCQUEVILLERS	2.12.15		A Draft of 1 Officer and 14 O.R. arrived from O.C. Reinforcement ETAPLES	
	3.12.15	10.30 a.m	L/Cpl Hughes Rifle wound in left hand. Weather very bad and trenches up to the waist in water. Patrol under Off Plackbook and 9/Lt Thompson went to the German Wire and reported it very thick no enemy replied to a sharp Grenade Bombardment. 9/Lt Plackbook and Sgt A.B. Wines awarded _____ Land by General Plumer for Distinguished Service. They proceeded with a party of 10 men below the crest of the Hill opposite S. FORTIN and placed the gun at point E.23.C.2.6. from where they fired the M.G. for two hours at & very working parties, and at their Front and Support Trenches opposite to BRAYELLE WOOD.	
	4.12.15		Enemy have been firing (Field Guns) intermittently during the day. Our Artillery replied heavily. 16 & 8 L/Cpl Simms wounded by Shrapnel in Right Arm.	

INTELLIGENCE SUMMARY.

(Erase heading not required.)

Place	Date	Hour	Summary of Events and Information	Remarks and references to Appendices
FONCQUEVILLERS	5.12.15		Weather continues very vile and Trenches flooded. Enemy Snipers very numerous in village on Artillery replied with good effect. Sgt B. Brook awarded Green Card for distinguished service when on Patrol with 2/Lt Koebbrick.	
"	6.12.15		1946 Pte Sullivan, 17506 Pte Worrall received Rifle wounds 16402 Pte J Brownlow killed in action. Enemy swept the trenches all day with Machine Gun fire and Rifle fire.	
"	7.12.15		Weather continues very bad and trenches are up to the waist in water, relief in the fire trenches take place by Company every 3 days owing to the weather, it being impossible for the men to stand the strain any longer.	
	8.12.15		The Battalion was relieved by the 10th Bn Royal Fusiliers. The leading Company of the Fusiliers arrived at FONCQUEVILLERS	

INTELLIGENCE SUMMARY.

(Erase heading not required.)

Place	Date	Hour	Summary of Events and Information	Remarks and references to Appendices
FONCQUEVILLERS	8-9.12.15		at 2.30pm Relief was completed at 5.20pm. The Battn marched to SOUASTRE to Billets	
SOUASTRE	10.12.15 to 19.12.15		The Battalion found fatigues every other day for repair of trenches at FONCQUEVILLERS and BIENVILLERS. 1 Sergeant and 30 men were sent to WARLINCOURT to Report to DIVISIONAL Train for Wood cutting	
FONCQUEVILLERS	20.12.15		The Battalion relieved the 10th Bn Royal Fusiliers, our leading Support Company arrived FONCQUEVILLERS at 2.30 pm relief was completed 5-7pm.	
	21.12.15		11354 Pte R.Seacock was wounded in action and Died of Wounds 21.12.15. Buried at HÉNU	
	22.12.15		The weather continues very bad and trenches impassable	

INTELLIGENCE SUMMARY.

(Erase heading not required.)

Place	Date	Hour	Summary of Events and Information	Remarks and references to Appendices
FONCQUEVILLERS	22.9.15		Reliefs by platoons are carried out every 24 hours. 14442 Sgt Allam was wounded in the thigh. 5938 Pte Young, while attempting to get Sgt Allam to a place of safety was severely wounded receiving a shattered fore arm. Pte Green assisted Pte Young to get Sgt Allam to a place of safety and Pte Young was given a Green Band by Major General Bount Stevens and Pte Young a Red band with remark to the effect that his conduct had been reported to Higher Authority.	
	23.12.15		A prisoner was caught on our wire by our sentries, another man of the same regiment as prisoner got away and wished to capture the other 16510 Pte Clery received a Rifle wound in right wrist.	
	24.12.15		Revd A.G. Hicks Service B.F. received Rifle wound in shoulder after having visited the troops in the trenches. 2093 Pte Boon	

INTELLIGENCE SUMMARY.
(Erase heading not required.)

Place	Date	Hour	Summary of Events and Information	Remarks and references to Appendices
FONQUEVILLERS 24/2/15			received a Rifle Wound in the Head. The enemy started Bombardment at 12.0 with Minenwerfer to several Hours and although much damage was done to the trenches only one casualty was reported 16.00 Pte Anderson being slightly wounded	
	25/2/15		Enemy continue to Bombard our trenches but only a few slight casualties occured these were able to return to duty after being attended to by our M.O.	
	26/2/15		16.09½ Pte Schofield 114982 Pte Renshaw both received Rifle wounds in Head and ear respectively both were admitted to Hospital. Patrols went out during the night and a large enemy patrol was met by 2/Lt Thompson and 8 men they Bombed the enemy patrol who retaliated with throwing bombs at our patrol no casualties occured to our nal and the	

INTELLIGENCE SUMMARY.

(Erase heading not required.)

Instructions regarding War Diaries and Intelligence Summaries are contained in F. S. Regs., Part II. and the Staff Manual respectively. Title pages will be prepared in manuscript.

Place	Date	Hour	Summary of Events and Information	Remarks and references to Appendices
FONCQUEVILLERS	26/12/15		Germans retired. The Brigadier General complimented 2/Lt Thompson on the good work of his patrol	
	27/12/15		There has been much Aeroplane activity during the last two days and enemy artillery dropped several shells in our trenches our Artillery replied vigorously, bombarding GOMMECOURT severely. Our front was patrolled throughout the night under Lt Warner, 2/Lt Bentley, 2/Lt Hollick, Sgt Shakeshaft and 2/Lt Rockrock. None of these patrols encountered any enemy patrols. Lt Warner took a Machine Gun out accompanied by 2/Lt Rockrock with covering party. They took lead the valley between the lines for 3 hours, without meeting anyone. The ground near the German lines is very swampy & in parts under water. While this patrol was out enemy machine gun opened fire. Rifle grenades were discharged at the German Machine Gun positions, our Machine Gun firing over the heads of our	

INTELLIGENCE SUMMARY.

(Erase heading not required.)

Summaries are contained in F.S. Regs., Part II. and the Staff Manual respectively. Title pages will be prepared in manuscript.

Place	Date	Hour	Summary of Events and Information	Remarks and references to Appendices
FONQUEVILLERS	28/12/15		takes at the machine gun positions. Enemy replied by throwing bombs from his front trench in addition to rifle and M.G. fire. The B.G.C. complimented this patrol for good work.	
	29/12/15		Enemy Artillery again bombarded ou. Trenches and the village of FONQUEVILLERS. Heavy Artillery bombarded the 2nd in retaliation. Enemy machine guns were active all day. Aeroplanes from both sides were observing for Artillery several attempts were made to bring them down but all were unsuccessful. Patrols were out during the night under Lt Fawcett, 2/Lieut Heath, Smith and Piggott none of these parties met any enemy patrols. Patrols report that enemy were heard working inside their trenches. 16599 Pte Lymers was wounded by shell.	
	30/12/15		Enemy Machine Gun fire was again active at stand to morning and night. There has been little Artillery fire on our front but heavy shells	

INTELLIGENCE / SUMMARY

(Erase heading not required.)

Place	Date	Hour	Summary of Events and Information	Remarks and references to Appendices
FONCQUEVILLERS	30/12/15		have landed on both our left and right. Patrols were out throughout the night under 2/Lt Heath, Humphreys, Leggett, Blair, and Smith, no enemy patrols were met. All patrols report the sound of trumping and talking going on in enemy trenches	
	31/12/15		Enemy Machine Guns very active. Our Artillery bombarded the enemy trenches from 12- 2 pm. Little reply was made. 9 O.R. Reinforcements arrived from 3rd Bn East Lancashire Regt. 16378 Pte Stoton was wounded in the head by shrapnel.	

112th Brigade.
37th Division

1/6th BATTALION EAST LANCASHIRE REGIMENT

JANUARY 1916 :::::::

WAR DIARY
or
INTELLIGENCE SUMMARY.

(Erase heading not required.)

Army Form C. 2118.

Place	Date	Hour	Summary of Events and Information	Remarks and references to Appendices
FONCQUEVILLER	1-1-16		The Battalion was relieved by the 10th Bn Royal Fusiliers relief by coys commenced at 3.0 pm and was completed about 6.0 pm. The Battalion proceeded to Rest Billets at SOUASTRE.	
SOUASTRE	2-1-16		6 Officers and 200 men proceeded to PAS to work under the Pioneer Battalion 9th North Staffordshire Regt.	
SOUASTRE	3-1-16		A draft of 96 other ranks arrived from the 3rd Bn East Lancashire Regt and were inspected by the Commanding Officer	
SOUASTRE	4-1-16		3 Officers + 100 Other Ranks proceeded to FONCQUEVILLERS for work on the repair of trenches this party was supplied daily. 2/Lt Bentley and 6 men were detailed by Brigade Office to work on Machine Gun Emplacements in the	

Army Form C. 2118.

WAR DIARY
or
INTELLIGENCE SUMMARY.
(Erase heading not required.)

Place	Date	Hour	Summary of Events and Information	Remarks and references to Appendices
SOUASTRE	4-1-16		Very Subsidiary Trench fine.	
SOUASTRE	5-1-16		In addition to FONCQUEVILLERS Working Party, 3 Officers and 150 Other Ranks worked in the Quarry at HENU, also 3 Officers and 150 Other Ranks were working on Brigade Grenade School near ST AMAND.	
SOUASTRE	6-1-16		Pte Doyle was accidentally wounded whilst practising Grenade throwing also Pte Briggs. 19506 Pte Hulse died in Hospital at BEAUVAL. 19751 Pte Goodwin was wounded whilst with Working Party at FONCQUEVILLERS.	
SOUASTRE	7-1-16		32 NCOs and men were interviewed regarding Munitions & were chosen for a test these men Proceeded to HAVRE.	

WAR DIARY
or
INTELLIGENCE SUMMARY.
(Erase heading not required.)

Army Form C. 2118.

Place	Date	Hour	Summary of Events and Information	Remarks and references to Appendices
SOUASTRE	8-1-16		While the Battalion were on the Parade ground the Germans fired several Shells on the ground. Pte Abraham being slightly wounded in the Head 2 others were partly damaged by the fall of Earth.	
SOUASTRE	9-1-16		An enemy Aeroplane dropped 3 Bombs on the Village doing no damage.	
SOUASTRE	13-1-16		The Battalion relieved the 10th Bn Royal Fusiliers at FONCQUEVILLERS relief was completed 6.25pm.	
FONCQUEVILLER	14-1-16		Situation has been very quiet since taking over from R Fus.	
	15-1-16		Enemy machine guns very active at Stand to night and morning. Enemy artillery active between 9.a.m. at 10 a Pte Wood being Killed and Pte Howarth badly wounded by Shell	

WAR DIARY
or
INTELLIGENCE SUMMARY.
(Erase heading not required.)

Army Form C. 2118.

Place	Date	Hour	Summary of Events and Information	Remarks and references to Appendices
FONCQUEVILLERS	16.1.16		Enemy very quiet all day excepting for Machine Gun fire at Stand To night and morning. Pte Breden Massey Wiltshire being wounded. Enemy artillery sent over several 77mm during the afternoon our Artillery replies effectively	
FONCQUEVILLERS	17.1.16		Enemy Aeroplane dropped 3 Bombs on our Right near the lines of the Warwickshire T.F. No material damage being observed.	
FONCQUEVILLERS	18.1.16		Cpl Mundin was wounded under the Heart and died of Wounds same day. Situation remains quiet between 7-8pm starting near MONCHY 3 Green rockets were sent up in rapid succession then after short interval this was repeated a little further South and was carried down the line to GOMMECOURT. Patrols were out under 2/Lts Bentley and Thompson but no enemy patrols were met. Lt Thompson and one man wate examining our wire	

Army Form C. 2118.

WAR DIARY
or
INTELLIGENCE SUMMARY.
(Erase heading not required.)

Instructions regarding War Diaries and Intelligence Summaries are contained in F. S. Regs., Part II. and the Staff Manual respectively. Title pages will be prepared in manuscript.

Place	Date	Hour	Summary of Events and Information	Remarks and references to Appendices
FONCQUEVILLERS	NOVEMBER 18.16		opposite Trench 54 when a patrol of about 12 Germans opened fire hitting 2/Lt Thompson in the ear. The Patrol then retired.	
	19.11.16		Situation quiet a noticeable feature has been the intermittent enemy M.G fire. An Enemy Trench Mortar which started firing from GOMMECOURT WOOD received in retaliation about a dozen shells to one fired by Trench Mortar which ceased firing after 3 rounds. The Mortar started again at 4.30 pm with same result. Patrols were out under Lt Peake Blair Humphreys on Smith. There were divided into two parties the first having reported that were fired on continually by M.G. Lt Peake was the only one hit being wounded slightly but able to resume command no enemy party was met.	
	20.11.16		Situation very quiet. Enemy snipers very active Sgt Bennett L/Cpl Knight and Pte Mammack being wounded. Patrols of 40 were out but met no enemy	

T2134. Wt. W708-776. 50000. 4/15. Sir J. C. & S.

WAR DIARY
or
INTELLIGENCE SUMMARY.
(Erase heading not required.)

Army Form C. 2118.

Instructions regarding War Diaries and Intelligence Summaries are contained in F. S. Regs., Part II. and the Staff Manual respectively. Title pages will be prepared in manuscript.

Place	Date	Hour	Summary of Events and Information	Remarks and references to Appendices
FONCQUEVILLERS	21-1-16		Situation quiet. Enemy M.G. active. Enemy artillery dropped a dozen shells into N.E. of FONCQUEVILLERS doing little damage. Our Artillery replied effectively. Pte Cartmell was wounded by M.G. fire. Patrols were out but nothing to Report. Pte Barlow was killed by M.G. fire.	
	22-1-16		Situation remains quiet. Enemy sent over 2 dozen 77 mm shells into our front line. Otherwise enemy artillery inactive. A large patrol was out under Lt Tuck but had nothing to report.	
	23-1-16		Situation Normal. Enemy Snipers very active also M.G. fire. Considerable Artillery activity on the part of the enemy about 3.0pm attention being confined to FONCQUEVILLERS. Patrols were out but nothing to report.	

WAR DIARY
or
INTELLIGENCE SUMMARY.
(Erase heading not required.)

Army Form C. 2118.

Place	Date	Hour	Summary of Events and Information	Remarks and references to Appendices
FONCQUEVILLERS	24-1-16		Situation quiet. About 40-77 mm shells fell in Souastre Square between 9-30 and 10-30. Casualties Nil.	
	25-1-16		Situation quiet excepting 2.0-3.30am. Between 2.0-3.0 am a violent Bombardment of our Trenches was carried out by the enemy, some 500 shells of all calibres including minenwerfer falling in our lines. Enemy M.G. fired intermittently throughout the night and kept up concentrated fire during the Bombardment. We had two casualties. Pte Darley being killed and Lpl Phillips being wounded. The Battalion was relieved by the 10th Bn Royal Fusiliers. The Batt. marched to SOUASTRE	
SOUASTRE	26-1-16		216 other Ranks proceeded to PAS for work whilst the Batt. is in Reserve. Lt Briggs and 20 men were attached to Brigade Grenade School for 10 days instruction.	

WAR DIARY
or
INTELLIGENCE SUMMARY.
(Erase heading not required.)

Army Form C. 2118.

Place	Date	Hour	Summary of Events and Information	Remarks and references to Appendices
SOUASTRE	27-1-16		The Battalion supplied 100 men daily for work on the Trenches at FONCQUEVILLERS	
	28-1-16		The Battalion was allotted the Sniping Range at GAUDIEMPRE and SOUASTRE.	
	29-1-16		30 Officers & 150 OR worked at Quarry at HENU. 100 Other Ranks worked for the Pioneer Battn 9th N.S. Regt.	
	31-1-16		The Battalion was allotted the Baths at PAS.	

112th Brigade.
37th Division.

1/8th BATTALION

EAST LANCASHIRE REGIMENT

FEBRUARY 1916

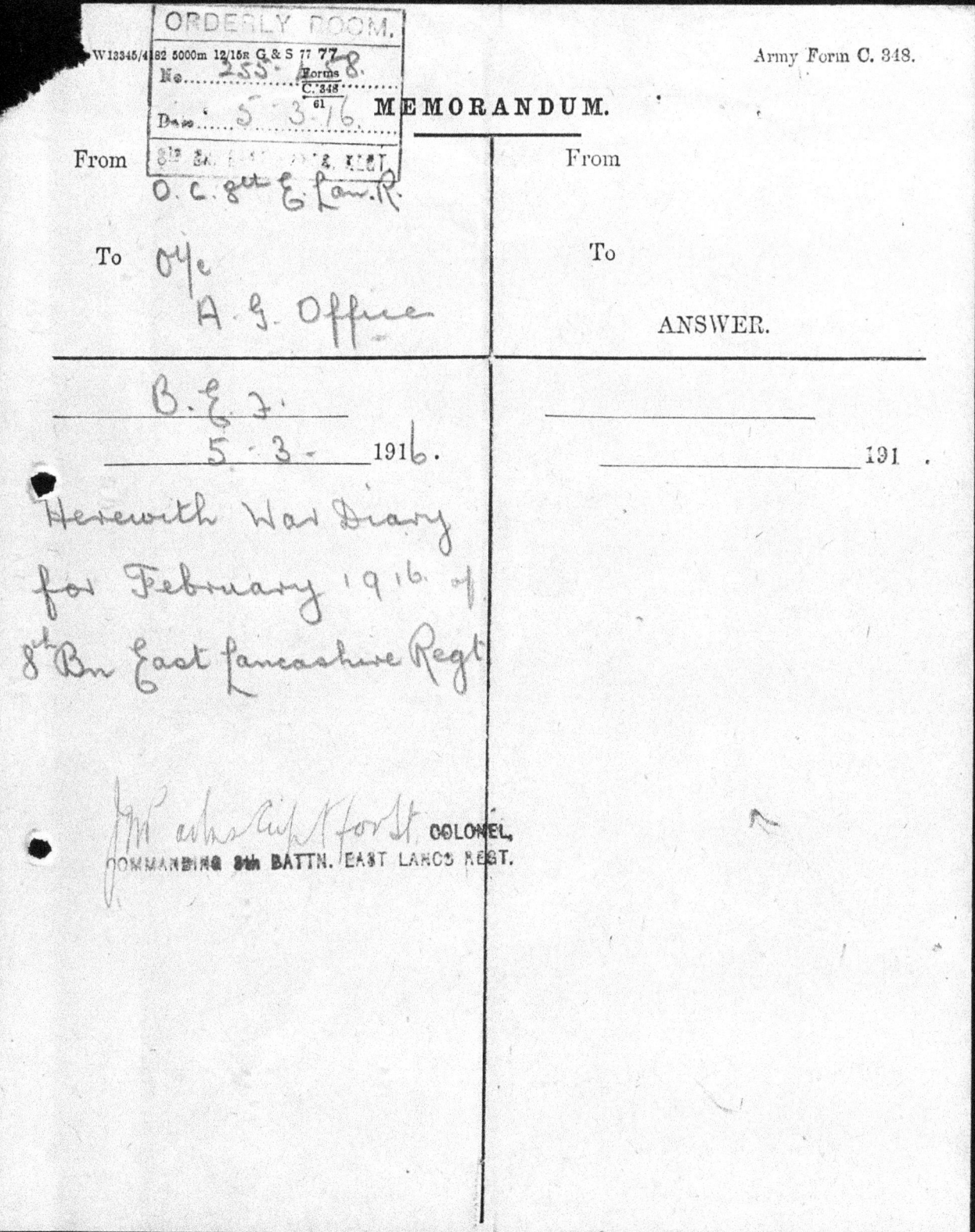

MEMORANDUM. Army Form C. 348.

From 8th Bn. East Lancs. Regt.
O.C. 8th E. Lan. R.

To O/c
A. G. Office

ORDERLY ROOM.
No. 255
Date 5-3-16

B.E.F.
5-3- 1916.

Herewith War Diary
for February 1916 of
8th Bn East Lancashire Regt.

J.W... Lieut for Lt. Colonel,
Commanding 8th Battn. East Lancs Regt.

37/112

37 8th E. Lancs:

Vol: 7

Feb. 1916

WAR DIARY
or
INTELLIGENCE SUMMARY.

(Erase heading not required.)

Army Form C. 2118.

Place	Date	Hour	Summary of Events and Information	Remarks and references to Appendices
SOUASTRE	1.2.16		The Battalion furnished Working Parties of 100 men for work on Trenches at FONCQUEVILLERS.	
"	4.2.16		The Battalion furnished Working Parties of 350 men for work on Trenches at FONCQUEVILLERS. and 100 men at QUARRY HENU. A Draft of 96 men joined from 3rd Battn.	
FONCQUEVILLERS	7.2.16		The Battalion relieved the 10th Bn Royal Fusiliers at FONCQUEVILLERS. The first Company arrived at 5.15 pm Relief completed 7.21 pm.	
"	8.2.16		Enemy Artillery very active ~200 shells of all calibres being fired at our Front line Trenches and Sixteen Square. Patrols were out under Pte Fawcett 2/Lt Humphreys and 2/Lt Smith no enemy patrol was met but 2 casualties sustained by M.G. fire which was very active all the night.	

Army Form C. 2118.

WAR DIARY
or
INTELLIGENCE SUMMARY.
(Erase heading not required.)

Instructions regarding War Diaries and Intelligence Summaries are contained in F.S. Regs., Part II. and the Staff Manual respectively. Title pages will be prepared in manuscript.

Place	Date	Hour	Summary of Events and Information	Remarks and references to Appendices
FONCQUEVILLERS	9.2.16		Enemy Artillery again very active 500 shells of all calibres being fired at our Batteries also Fire and Support Trenches. 5 casualties were sustained. Patrols were out under Lt Fawcett, Stock, Smith, and Beloe, nothing to report.	
	10.2.16		Enemy artillery fairly active 400 shells being fired at our Fire and Support Trenches. 3 casualties were reported. Patrols were out all night but no enemy patrols were met.	
	11.2.16		Enemy Artillery not so active some 120 shells of various calibre being dropped in Village of FONCQUEVILLERS and Support Trenches Patrols were out but no enemy were met.	
	12.2.16		Enemy 15 Pounder Trench Mortar fired 100 shells in our front line. A large number of Green Rockets were sent up all along the line commencing in front of ESSART and finishing at GOMMECOURT no action	

T2134. Wt. W708–776. 500000. 4/15. Sir J.C. & S.

Army Form C. 2118.

WAR DIARY
or
INTELLIGENCE SUMMARY.
(Erase heading not required.)

Instructions regarding War Diaries and Intelligence Summaries are contained in F. S. Regs., Part II. and the Staff Manual respectively. Title pages will be prepared in manuscript.

Place	Date	Hour	Summary of Events and Information	Remarks and references to Appendices
FONCQUEVILLERS	12.2.16		followed. Patrols were out under Lt Snelle and 2/Lt Piggott nothing to report.	
	13.2.16		The Battalion was relieved by 7th Bn Worcester Regt. Relief was completed at 7.30pm. The Battalion moves to Bart Billets at HUMBERCAMPS.	
HUMBERCAMPS	15.2.16		Working Parties were found for work on Trenches at BERLES. also Parties for work on Quarries were found.	
"	18.2.16		The Battalion relieved the 1st Bn Lincoln Regt at BERLES. Relief was completed at 8.15 am.	
BERLES. S.	19.2.16		Enemy Snipers were very active all day. Captain G. Hammond and Pte A.B. Winser being wounded.	

T2134. Wt. W708-776. 500030. 1/15. Sir J. C. & S.

WAR DIARY
or
INTELLIGENCE SUMMARY.
(Erase heading not required.)

Army Form C. 2118.

Place	Date	Hour	Summary of Events and Information	Remarks and references to Appendices
BERLES	22.2.16		The Battalion was relieved by 6th Leicester Regt. Relief was completed at 9-15 hrs. The Battalion proceeded to Rest Billets at HUMBERCAMPS.	
HUMBERCAMPS	23.2.16		The Battalion found working Parties for 110th Inf Bde. for work on Trenches at BERLES.	
	23.2.16		The Battalion proceeded to BIENVILLERS as support battalion to 112 Brigade at HANNESCAMPS, relieving the 1/4 T. Bn Gloucester Regt.	
	24.2.16		The Battalion found working Parties for 10th Bn Loyal N. Lancs. and 11th Bn R. Warwicks Regt at HANNESCAMPS.	

112th Brigade.
37th Division.

1/8th BATTALION

EAST LANCASHIRE REGIMENT

MARCH 1 9 1 6

8 East Lancs WAR DIARY
or
INTELLIGENCE SUMMARY.

Army Form C. 2118.

(Erase heading not required.)

Place	Date	Hour	Summary of Events and Information	Remarks and references to Appendices
HUMBERCAMPS	1-3-16		Working Parties were found for work in Trenches at HANNESCAMPS for the 10th L.N. Lancs and 11th Bn R Warwicks Regt. daily	
HANNESCAMPS	6-3-16		The Battalion relieved the 10th Bn L.N. Lancs in the Trenches at HANNESCAMPS. Relief was commenced at 5-15 pm and completed by 9-15 pm	
	8-3-16		17193 Pte J.E. Heys was killed by Shell. Enemy very quiet and hardly a shot fired	
FONCQUEVILLERS	9-3-16		The Battalion took over the Trenches at FONCQUEVILLERS from the 48th Division. The Trenches were in a very bad condition and very little wire in front of the Firing Line.	
	12-3-16		The Battalion was relieved by the 10th Bn Royal N. Lancs. proceeding to Rest Billets at POMMIER	

WAR DIARY
or
INTELLIGENCE SUMMARY.

(Erase heading not required.)

Army Form C. 2118.

Place	Date	Hour	Summary of Events and Information	Remarks and references to Appendices
POMMIER	14.3.16		Working Parties were found for rebuilding the Corps Line	
	16.3.16		The Battalion attended a Trench Mortar demonstration at V.12.c.9.3. North of LA CAUCHIE.	
	17.3.16		The Battalion less "C" Coy with 2 Platoons of "D" Coy proceeded to MONDICOURT, C.Coy with part of "D" Coy proceeded to LAHERLIERE. working Parties were found daily at these Places.	
	25.3.16		The Battalion moved to ST AMAND and were joined there by the Detachment from LAHERLIERE.	
	27.3.16		Working Parties of 500 men were detailed for work on the Corps Line. This Party was detailed daily.	

112th Brigade.
37th Division.

1/8th BATTALION

EAST LANCASHIRE REGIMENT

APRIL 1916

ORDERLY ROOM.
No. 16 C.
Date 29-5-16.
8th Bn. EAST LANCS.

To. O/C A.G. Office

Herewith War diary
of 8th Bn East Lancashire
Regt.

J. Parks Capt
for Lt Colonel,
COMMANDING 8th BATTN EAST LANCS REGT.

April. 1916

WAR DIARY
or
INTELLIGENCE SUMMARY.
(Erase heading not required.)

Army Form C. 2118.

XXXVII 8 E Lans
1/OP.

Place	Date	Hour	Summary of Events and Information	Remarks and references to Appendices
ST AMAND	1-4-16		Working Parties were found daily for Work on Corps Line.	
	9-4-16		The Battalion moved to rest Billets at SUS. ST. LEGER. moving via GAUDIEMPRÉ.	
	10-4-16		The Battalion attended a Flame demonstration at N.28. & 9.3. (S.W of Sus ST LEGER)	
	11-4-16		The Battalion paraded for Bombing Drill daily	
	16-4-16		B Coy were allotted the Range at LUCHEUX	
	16-4-16		Bombing practise in advancing in Artillery Formation etc.	
	17-4-16		A Coy paraded for practise Bombing attack under Lt MacQueen	

Army Form C. 2118.

WAR DIARY
or
INTELLIGENCE SUMMARY.
(Erase heading not required.)

Place	Date	Hour	Summary of Events and Information	Remarks and references to Appendices
SUS St LEGER	18.4.16		B Coy allotted Range T.6.c.	Maps 51.c.
	19.4.16		Companies Paraded for Drill in close and open order, opening out to Artillery formation etc, daily	
	20.4.16		The Battalion attended a Smoke demonstration at S.O.S. Grenade School.	
	9.4.16		Battalion Route March. Route :- SUS, GRAND RULLECOURT - LIENCOURT - LE CAUROY.	"
	9.4.16		Working Parties were found daily for hurdle making in LUCHEUX & ROBERMONT Woods.	
	30.4.16		The Battalion moved to SOUASTRE.	

112th Brigade.

37th Division.

1/8th BATTALION

EAST LANCASHIRE REGIMENT

M A Y 1 9 1 6

ORDERLY ROOM.
No. 399A
Date 2-7-16
8TH BN. EAST LANCS. REGT.

To O.i/c A.G.s Office

Herewith Intelligence Summary
8th (S). Bn East Lancashire Regt.

Hector L Billinger
2/Lieut A/Adjt
For Lt Colonel
COMMANDING 8th BATTN. EAST LANCS REGT

[827] W13345..182 5000m 12,15k G & S 77 **MEMORANDUM.** Army Form C. 348

ORDERLY ROOM.
No. 116 A
8th Bn. EAST LANCS. REGT.

From O.C.
8th Bn E Lan R.

To D.A.G.
G.H.Q.

From

To

ANSWER

4-6- 1916.

Herewith War Diary
for May 1916
8th Bn East Lancashire Regt

J Marks Capt
for Lt Colonel
COMMANDING 8th BATTN. EAST LANCS. REGT.

_____ 191

8 East 32/12

Army Form C. 2118.
Vol 10

WAR DIARY
or
INTELLIGENCE SUMMARY. XXXVII

(Erase heading not required.)

Instructions regarding War Diaries and Intelligence Summaries are contained in F.S. Regs., Part II. and the Staff Manual respectively. Title pages will be prepared in manuscript.

10-X
7 shuts

Place	Date	Hour	Summary of Events and Information	Remarks and references to Appendices
SOOASTRE	2-5-16		A draft of 14 other Ranks regressed from 37 Inf Base Depot. The Battalion proceeded to the trenches at FONCQUEVILLERS to relieve 2nd Bn Royal Irish Regiment. Relief commenced at 8-15 p.m. and completed by 10-25 p.m. Patrols were sent out, but with exception of hearing a wiring party at S.2, nothing was heard of the enemy.	Ref/59P N.E.1946-47
FONCQUEVILLERS	3-5-16		Enemy bombarded our Left Company with about 150. 15cm shells falling in rear of trenches. Enemy periodically traverses our positions with Machine Gun Fire. 1905 2nd Lieut Tattersall was killed by Shell wound. 1428 Pte Smith, 1716 Lce Cpl Beech 1456 Cpl Robertson were killed and 1765 Pte Sargent, Pte Franklin, Pte Matthews and Pte Toulson Wounded by Enemy Explosion.	
	4-5-16		Enemy quiet and little to report. Heavy horse & Motor Transport could be heard moving towards LA BRAYELLE Farm at 9-15 pm until 10-30 pm. Pte Corless received Rifle wound in knee.	

T2134. Wt. W708—770. 500000. 4/15. Sir J.C. & S.

Army Form C. 2118.

WAR DIARY
or
INTELLIGENCE SUMMARY.
(Erase heading not required.)

Instructions regarding War Diaries and Intelligence Summaries are contained in F.S. Regs., Part II. and the Staff Manual respectively. Title pages will be prepared in manuscript.

Place	Date	Hour	Summary of Events and Information	Remarks and references to Appendices
FONCQUEVILLERS	5-5-16		Enemy artillery fairly active. Firing about 65 – 77mm Shells in Sniper Square. A few Bursts from Machine Guns at "Stand To"	
"	6-5-16		Situation quiet. Transport heard in direction of Ja Brayelle Road between 9.30 and 10.30 p.m. Several snipings were taken from a Board hut between the Lines.	
"	7-5-16		The 48th Division Artillery Shelled Transport on SOMMECOURT – ESSARTS Rd. The Enemy retaliated sending 20 or 30 shells into W of FONCQUEVILLERS. Our Artillery obtained a direct hit on M.G. Emplacement.	
"	8-5-16		Unusually quiet. Several Patrols were out during the night but none of the Enemy were met. Enemy fired showers of Rounds of S.A.A at our Aeroplanes. L/Cpl Evans + Pte Hunt wounded.	

T2134. Wt. W708-776. 500000. 4/15. Sir J.C. & S.

Army Form C. 2118.

WAR DIARY
or
INTELLIGENCE SUMMARY.
(Erase heading not required.)

Instructions regarding War Diaries and Intelligence Summaries are contained in F.S. Regs., Part II. and the Staff Manual respectively. Title pages will be prepared in manuscript.

Place	Date	Hour	Summary of Events and Information	Remarks and references to Appendices
FONCQUEVILLERS	10.5.16		Very little activity all day. A few bursts from Machine Gun were fired after stand to. A mule No 5 Grenade was fired from a Rifle into the Poplar. The Enemy sent up 2 Flares but nothing further occurred. The Battalion was relieved by the 6th N. Stafford Regt. The Battalion proceeded to HANNESCAMPS	
HANNESCAMPS	11.5.16		The Battalion took over Trenches 64 to 79 inclusive, from 10th Bn. K.N. Lanc and 11th R Warwicks.	
	12.5.16		Enemy Artillery very active all along our Front. Machine Guns fairly active all day. Pte Hutchinson Killed, Pte Hutton and Oxnard Wounded by shell.	
	13.5.16		Artillery Quiet about 30 Trench Mortar bombs were fired into our Front Line Trenches. Machine Guns fairly active. Sgt Smith Wounded.	

Army Form C. 2118.

WAR DIARY
or
INTELLIGENCE SUMMARY.
(Erase heading not required.)

Instructions regarding War Diaries and Intelligence Summaries are contained in F.S. Regs., Part II. and the Staff Manual respectively. Title pages will be prepared in manuscript.

Place	Date	Hour	Summary of Events and Information	Remarks and references to Appendices
HANNESCAMPS	1.5.16		Artillery very quiet. Very little Machine Gun fire only at our Aircraft. 80 French Mortar Bombs were sent over falling near Pillen Tree Corner, a good deal of damage was done to the trench. The Battalion was relieved by the 9th Bn Leinster Regt. and proceeded to BAYINCOURT	
BAYINCOURT	1.5.16 3.5.16		The Battalion found working parties between 500 and 600 strong for work on Redoubts between BERLES and POMMIER	
HANNESCAMPS	2.5.16		The Battalion relieved the 9th Bn Leinster Regt. Enemy Artillery quiet, Little Machine Gun fire. Patrols were out but nothing to Report.	
	3/5/16		Artillery active shells of all calibres falling behind our trenches & Rifle Grenades hit the traverse of our trenches 76-77	

WAR DIARY
or
INTELLIGENCE SUMMARY.
(Erase heading not required.)

Army Form C. 2118.

Place	Date	Hour	Summary of Events and Information	Remarks and references to Appendices
HANNESCAMPS	28.1.16		Enemy registered new Sap running from Trench 73. Enemies Artillery activity 200 shells of all calibres on Fuller Tree Corner & Trench 73. Free Machine Gun activity. No hostile patrols observed. A large working party carried on work of new trench from the head of Sap 73. Enemy fired about 25. 77mm shells at various times but did little damage. Pte Williamson, Pte Stubbs and Pte Hutton wounded.	
	29.5/16		Enemy Artillery active about 150 shells of all calibre falling on trenches 74 & 75. Obtaining several direct hits on the Parados. Machine Guns very quiet. A Patrol was out to try and locate the position from which flares were sent up since the enemy's line just N.E. of the MONCHY Rd. The Patrol returned about midnight. No flares were sent up while the Patrol was out. Casualties Pte Dobson, Pte Cox. wounded Shell	

Army Form C. 2118.

WAR DIARY
or
INTELLIGENCE SUMMARY.
(Erase heading not required.)

Instructions regarding War Diaries and Intelligence Summaries are contained in F. S. Regs., Part II. and the Staff Manual respectively. Title pages will be prepared in manuscript.

Place	Date	Hour	Summary of Events and Information	Remarks and references to Appendices
HANNESCAMP	30.5.16		Artillery Normal. Machine Guns traversed on Parados from Trenches 95 to 99 several times causing our Working Parties to cease.	
	31.5.16		Enemy Artillery more active. Machine guns little activity. Trenches 96 and 99 were traversed at intervals. Casualties 2/Lt Smith E.B. Rifle Wound in R Hand.	

T2134. Wt. W708–776. 500096. 4/15. Sir J. C. & S.

112th Brigade.
37th Division.

Battalion went to 34th Division 5th July 1916.
Rejoined 37th Division 21st August 1916.

1/8th BATTALION

EAST LANCASHIRE REGIMENT

JUNE 1916

Army Form C. 2118.

Vol 11
37/112
June

11.X
what

WAR DIARY
or
INTELLIGENCE SUMMARY.
(Erase heading not required.)

XXXVII

Place	Date	Hour	Summary of Events and Information	Remarks and references to Appendices
HANNESCAMP	1-6-16		Fair artillery. No Registration. The enemy put three shells calibre 5.9" on HANNESCAMP-BIENVILLERS Rd by Battn H.Qrs. Some damage was done and casualties occurred.	
	2-6-16		Enemy Artillery more active. Machine guns between 9.45am 1-0 a gun firing directly from a point opposite trench 68 gave some trouble to our working and covering party in S. of 12, and but in its aim had entirely been forsaken. We had no casualty. Major B. H.O Mayrott was killed by Shell. 5 Boyle Brown. A. was seriously wounded	
	3-6-16		Enemy artillery fairly active. Machine Guns showed little activity only at Avocet. A covering party in front of Trench 1/2 saw a small German patrol crossing their Front halfway across the front of our Sonnen. They halted about 10 minutes they kept close to their own wire. Pte Kearns killed	

WAR DIARY
or
INTELLIGENCE SUMMARY.
(Erase heading not required.)

Army Form C. 2118.

Instructions regarding War Diaries and Intelligence Summaries are contained in F. S. Regs, Part II. and the Staff Manual respectively. Title pages will be prepared in manuscript.

Place	Date	Hour	Summary of Events and Information	Remarks and references to Appendices
HANNESCAMPS.			Artillery firing quiet. 80 – 150 mm shells were dropped in neighbourhood of full Lane. 30.77 mm shells have fallen at various times in our sector. Machine Guns very quiet all day. Enemy Working Parties observed working on their second line opposite French 7th. Naval Transport was heard behind MONCHY and ESSARTS.	
"	5-6-16		Enemy Artillery firing active. Pte Hurst and Pte McBrity were wounded by shells. Machine Guns quiet all day. Patrols were out nothing to Report	
"	6.6.16		Enemy Artillery very quiet. The Battalion was Relieved by 9th Leicester Regt. Relief commenced at 10·45 p.m and completed at 1·18 a.m 7th inst. B. C. & D Coys. remained at BIENVILLERS and HANNESCAMPS for work for R.F.A and work on Trenches. 2 Platoons of A Coy remained at BIENVILLERS with D Coy. Battalion Headqtrs with 2 Platoons of A Coy moved to BAVINCOURT	

Army Form C. 2118.

WAR DIARY
or
INTELLIGENCE SUMMARY.
(Erase heading not required.)

Instructions regarding War Diaries and Intelligence Summaries are contained in F. S. Regs., Part II. and the Staff Manual respectively. Title pages will be prepared in manuscript.

Place	Date	Hour	Summary of Events and Information	Remarks and references to Appendices
BAVINCOURT	7.6.16		Working Parties were found for R.E. and Town Commandant daily.	
	10.6.16		50 more men with 2/Lt Humphries were sent as further working party to BIENVILLERS for work on Reserve Redoubts Trenches	
	11.6.16		Working Parties were found for R.B.3.A. and R.E.s	
BIENVILLERS	16.6.16		Working Parties were employed carrying gas appliances to Trenches at Hannescamps & Berles	
BIENVILLERS	17.6.16		Carrying Parties again found for carrying gas Trench appliances	
BAVINCOURT	18.6.16		Battalion proceeded by Companies to Relieve 9th Leicesters at Hannescamps. "B" Coy left at 8.15 p.m. Companies leaving at intervals. Relief was completed at 1.45 a.m. Enemy Artillery very quiet. Machine guns traversed on harassed drumming	

Army Form C. 2118.

WAR DIARY
or
INTELLIGENCE SUMMARY.
(Erase heading not required.)

Instructions regarding War Diaries and Intelligence Summaries are contained in F.S. Regs., Part II. and the Staff Manual respectively. Title pages will be prepared in manuscript.

Place	Date	Hour	Summary of Events and Information	Remarks and references to Appendices
HANNESCAMPS	19.6.16		the night in Trenches 75-79. Otherwise very little activity.	SYDNE.182
"	20.6.16		Enemy artillery more active. Trenches 74 & 79 & Support line and communication Trenches Regulieu. New Bottain thought to have been brought up, some damage done to Scotfire Trenches 3 casualties. Enemy trench mining. But owing to our own working parties we were unable to fire. Heavy Transport could be heard entering MONCHY. Lights frequent seen in neighbourhood of Queens Ave & gaotes.	"
"	21.6.16		Enemy Artillery fairly active. 50 – 4.2 Shells were fired on Trenches 70 to 75. no damage was done. Machine Guns very quiet, enemy frequently towered our Right Section between 12–2 am. Pte Ackers wounded. Our Bombing/Training Party initially being heard. A German Patrol were seen by our covering party near the ravine, they made no attempt to approach our lines. The Enemy were heard working between his front an supports line opposite our Right Company. A large party joined up the New Trench 66–70 and running some. A few Shells were fired at the without doing any damage. Enemy Transport heard approaching MONCHY. A great deal of noise & shouting was heard behind Enemy Frontline.	"

Army Form C. 2118.

WAR DIARY
or
INTELLIGENCE SUMMARY.
(*Erase heading not required.*)

Instructions regarding War Diaries and Intelligence Summaries are contained in F.S. Regs., Part II. and the Staff Manual respectively. Title pages will be prepared in manuscript.

Place	Date	Hour	Summary of Events and Information	Remarks and references to Appendices
HANNESCAMPS	22.6.16		Enemy Artillery generally quiet. Few shells have fallen in our lines during the past 24 hours. 10 heavy trench Mortar Bombs were fired into Trench 94 & support lines. Machine Gun traverses on parapet during the day. Enemy working Party were observed harassing sun. The Enemy's front line early in the morning carrying timber. Our Snipers accounted for one of the Enemy who exposed themselves opposite Trench 94. Enemy shouting from their trenches "Come on" several times during the night.	5/D.N.E.112
"	23.6.16		Enemy artillery quiet, a number of heavy shells were fired over our lines in the direction of BIENVILLERS. Several Rifle Grenades were fired into Trenches 96 & 99. Machine Guns showed little activity. Aerial booted enemy parties working on the mine S. of MONCHY. Ra with considerable was also in progress in the Enemy's Front line, it was to have moving planks about and digging. Working Parties were fired on continually by our Lewis Guns. Enemy in good spirits, shouting and singing a whistling as they worked. Motor Transport was heard moving from Essarts to Monchy. Work on our lines was carried on in New Trench & Evening supplements to an addition.	

Place	Date	Hour	Summary of Events and Information	Remarks and references to Appendices
HANNESCAMPS	24.6.16		Enemy Artillery quiet. 50 77mm shells fired at various times at places in our Sector. Machine Guns show little activity. 1 Rfl Gr'y wounded. Enemy increasing trenches in front on by our Lewis Guns. Rumour Situation quiet. 50 Rifle Grenades fired in trenches 96&97 without doing any damage. Enemy discontinued firing after our Artillery burst a few rounds of shrapnel over his lines. Gas appliances continued to be stored in our lines also new trench mortars on Weather very wet.	S7D N.E./92.
"	25.6.16		Little more than usual Artillery excepting for a number of Heavy Trench Mortar bombs that in front of Trench 95. a good number of 77-mm shells were fired during the same period. Our Lewis Guns have very active on points where working Parties were observed. The Enemy sent many flares up during the night. Our snipers claim to have shot six of the Enemy.	"
"	26.6.16		Enemy Artillery quiet with the exception of a few Heavy Trench Mortar bombs in the Trenches 95-97. Enemy Machine Guns fairly active. Enemy strengthening his Safe at	"

Army Form C. 2118.

WAR DIARY
or
INTELLIGENCE SUMMARY.
(Erase heading not required.)

Instructions regarding War Diaries and Intelligence Summaries are contained in F. S. Regs., Part II. and the Staff Manual respectively. Title pages will be prepared in manuscript.

Place	Date	Hour	Summary of Events and Information	Remarks and references to Appendices
HANNESCAMPS	27.1.16	E.11.d.10.23.	General situation quiet. A recceing party sent patrol had nothing to Report. The Enemy quieted down no visibility or artillery being heard. An enemy aeroplane observed to make a sudden descent in direction of Adinfer woods after a fight with two of our Aircraft. Same was missed from trenches 94 to 93. Enemy artillery being busy after the aeroplane incident trenches 94 to 96 Heavies & Quarters. Enough firing mostly little activity after the first time. There was considerable gun firing was intermittent his machine guns were frequently sent his machine guns were frequently heard of the night.	57/AN.E.12.
	28.1.16		Enemy Artillery very active Trenches 96 to 97 were the enemy's principal target with a considerable amount of various calibres and Heavy Trench Mortars bombs to destroy a considerable amount of damage with the latter in Dead End. Nearly 500 pd and 77 m shells were fired into village of HANNESCAMPS and communication trenches at LUZLANES WORMWOOD AVENUE. New Trenches were observed working in Enemy's lines Patrols sent out what Enemy was quiet No Transport was heard. Enemy continually sent up flares during the night.	

T2134. Wt. W708-778. 500000. 4/15. Sir J. C. & S.

WAR DIARY
or
INTELLIGENCE SUMMARY.
(Erase heading not required.)

Army Form C. 2118.

Place	Date	Hour	Summary of Events and Information	Remarks and references to Appendices
HANNESCAMPS	29.6.16		Sun was emitted again at 11.0 am very little enemy Rifle & Machine Gun fire. Artillery heavily bombed our trenches at enemy several kills in our trenches. 4 O.R. being killed and 8 O.R. being wounded. Patrols out at night met no Enemy Patrols. Four Scouts were but in enemy territory but at E.11.b.2.2. without knowing any response but there were seen at the 2 solos near Admiral Wood.	57D/N.E.1 & 2.
	30.6.16		Only normal activity, a few 77 m.m. shells have been fired into our front line & communication trenches. General Situation quiet. Officers Patrol nothing to Report. Machine Gun fairly active.	

112th Brigade.
37th Division.
34th Division from 5.7.16.

Transferred with 112th Brigade from
37th Division to 34th Division 5.7.16.

8th
~~2nd~~ BATTALION

EAST LANCASHIRE REGIMENT

JULY 1916

WAR DIARY or INTELLIGENCE SUMMARY

Army Form C. 2118.

Vol 12

Place	Date	Hour	Summary of Events and Information	Remarks and references to Appendices
HANNESCAMPS	1-7-16		At 7.25am the Battalion discharged a covering Smoke Cloud. Germans opened Rifle fire and a Heavy Bartangeon Barrage. Everything was quiet by 9.30am. Enemy shelled our own trenches with S.A.A. Battalion killed 8 wounded.	
	2-7-16		Day quiet. Battalion relieved by 5th Bn Lincoln Regt. Relief completed 1-20am. Battalion proceeded to Bivouacs at Pommier.	
	3.7.16		Bivouacs at Pommier.	
POMMIER	4.7.16		Battalion marched to HALLOY, leaving POMMIER 10.0am arrived at PAS. Leaving HALLOY 2.40pm.	
HALLOY	5.7.16		Battalion Rested in Billets.	
"	6.7.16		Battalion entrained in Busses at 11.0am and proceeded to MILLENCOURT arriving at 4 – 0 pm and joined 34 Division.	
MILLENCOURT	6.7.16 6.0am		Battalion marched to BELLE VUE FARM Nr ALBERT arriving at 9.30am.	
"	7.7.16		Battalion proceeded to TARA-USNA LINE by Companies at 15 minutes intervals.	

Army Form C. 2118.

WAR DIARY
or
INTELLIGENCE SUMMARY.
(Erase heading not required.)

Instructions regarding War Diaries and Intelligence Summaries are contained in F.S. Regs., Part II. and the Staff Manual respectively. Title pages will be prepared in manuscript.

Place	Date	Hour	Summary of Events and Information	Remarks and references to Appendices
BECOURT WOOD	6.7		The night 6-7 was spent under most trying conditions in the Open.	
	7.7.16		The Battalion proceeded to Reserve Trenches in HELIGOLAND. Relieving the 9 Cheshire Regt.	
HELIGOLAND	9.7.16		Battalion supplied carrying parties for front & support lines. Enemy Artillery very active until	
	10.7.16		11 a.m. 10.5 mm during daylight & every night to fine Fragmentary Shells, while we were in these Trenches.	
CLOSE SUPPORT	11.7.16		The Battalion moved up to close support Relieving 6 Bedford Regt. commencing at 10 p.m.	
	12.		Repairing Trenches and watching fire Slips & enemy Artillery active causing several Casualties. On the 14th	
	13			
	13-14		Battalion relieved 10 Bn Royal N Lancs Regt in front line.	
	16.7.16	3.0 am	At 3.0 am Lt MacQueen took out Patrol of 6 Grenadiers, 1 Platoon and Lewis Gun Section and advanced about 500 yards	

WAR DIARY
or
INTELLIGENCE SUMMARY.

Army Form C. 2118.

Place	Date	Hour	Summary of Events and Information	Remarks and references to Appendices
	4/9/16		from our front line towards POZIERES epating trench there. 2/Lt Lightbound A. at the same time took a reconnoitring patrol out to the enemy lines. position at point 97, about 200 yards from POZIERES. 1/12/2/125 line which was afterwards held by 2/Lt Brunnell and Speak with 6 Grenadiers 1 Platoon 1 Lewis Gun Section at 4.0 pm Lt Macqueen's Party, was relieved by 2/Lt Stout with 6 Grenadiers 1 Platoon 1 Lewis Gun Section at 7.0 pm 2/Lt Stout with his party attempted to enter POZIERES. the party arrived at the Barriers on the POZIERES-ALBERT ROAD where 3 Germans were seen. 2 were bayonetted by our men but the third escaped and gave the Alarm. Our party then had to retire receiving very heavy casualties from Machine Guns situated in the Houses and Orchards around POZIERES	

WAR DIARY
or
INTELLIGENCE SUMMARY.
(Erase heading not required.)

Army Form C. 2118.

Place	Date	Hour	Summary of Events and Information	Remarks and references to Appendices
POZIERES	15.7.16		At 9.20 am after heavy bombardment of POZIERES for one hour, the Battalion led a Brigade Attack on the Village. A & B Coys in the Front Line, C & D Coys in Support. Owing to Artillery Barrage and Machine Gun Fire the Battalion was unable to achieve its objective but ――― was joined by the Units of the Brigade and consolidated existing trenches to East and South East of POZIERES. At 5.0 pm a further bombardment of POZIERES was carried out and the Battalion with Remainder Brigade attempted another assault on POZIERES at 6-8 pm, this assault was again held up by Machine Gun and Wire not being cut in the Hedges surrounding the Village. The Battalion handed over the Trenches to the 10th Bn Royal North Lancashire Regt at 2.30 am, and proceeded to Trenches in Blqus Support. Casualties Officers Killed 1 Ord Ranks Killed 56. Wounded 8. Other Ranks Wounded 276 Missing 33.	

WAR DIARY
or
INTELLIGENCE SUMMARY

(Erase heading not required.)

Army Form C. 2118.

Place	Date	Hour	Summary of Events and Information	Remarks and references to Appendices
CLOSE SUPPORT	16th		The Battalion was relieved by the Northumberland Fusiliers Battalion at 3.15 p.m. The Battalion proceeded to Billets in ALBERT.	
ALBERT	17th		The Battalion rested in ALBERT.	
BRESLE	18th		at 6.0 p.m. the Battalion moved to BRESLE.	
	19th		The Battalion moved to Billets in LA HOUSSOYE.	
BEHENCOURT	21st		The Battalion marched to Billets in BEHENCOURT where training of Specialists was continued until 29th inst.	
B.	25th		Battalion was reinforced by 7 Officers 170 Other Ranks. Other Ranks detained at FRECHINCOURT.	
	26th		The Brigade was inspected by Lt. Gen. Sir W.P. Pulteney K.C.B. D.S.O. Commanding "—" Corps. In his address to the Brigade, the General complimented all Ranks on their gallantry and devotion to duty in the recent fighting around POZIERES	
	26th 27th		The Reinforcements joined Battalion about 8.0 p.m. The Commanding Officers inspected the new draft of 170 O.R.	

Army Form C. 2118.

WAR DIARY
or
INTELLIGENCE SUMMARY.
(Erase heading not required.)

Instructions regarding War Diaries and Intelligence Summaries are contained in F. S. Regs., Part II. and the Staff Manual respectively. Title pages will be prepared in manuscript.

Place	Date	Hour	Summary of Events and Information	Remarks and references to Appendices
BERTRANCOURT	30/6		The Battalion commenced the march to BECOURT WOOD spending night 30-31st at BRESLE.	
	31/6	6.30 pm	At 6.30 pm march continued to BECOURT WOOD where Battalion Bivouacked in Reserve area.	

M Mackay Lt Col

112th Brigade.
34th Division till 21st August.
rejoined -37th Division. 21st August 1916.

Battalion rejoined 37th Division 21.8.16

1/8th BATTALION

EAST LANCASHIRE REGIMENT

AUGUST 1916

ORDERLY ROOM.
No. 763A
Date 3-9-16
8TH BN. EAST LANCS. REGT.

Confidential

War Diary

of

8th (S). Bn. East Lancashire Regt.

From 1-8-16.   To. 31-8-16

Volume 13.

J D Mackay
COMMANDING 8th BATTN. EAST LANCS REGT
LT. COLONEL

rejoined 37th Div
21/8/16

WAR DIARY

or

INTELLIGENCE SUMMARY

(Erase heading not required.)

Army Form C. 2118.

Place	Date	Hour	Summary of Events and Information	Remarks and references to Appendices
BECOURT WOOD	1st August 1916		The battalion remained in bivouac area at BECOURT WOOD until 4th August. A draft of 84 reinforcements joined the battalion on the 3rd August.	
	4/8/16		On this date in the early afternoon the battalion moved up to a line of support trenches running in front of the QUADRANGLE. While in this position, on the night of the 5th-6th the battalion suffered some casualties from German heavy artillery, which was searching for the numerous gun positions in the vicinity.	
	7/8/16		The battalion proceeded to relieve the 15th Bn Royal Scots in trenches in front of BAZENTIN-le-PETIT. In this position the left company (G Coy) shared a trench with the enemy and were separated from him by two barriers. A company was organised on the night of the 7th-8th August with the object of capturing as much as possible of that part of the trench held by the enemy. Two bombing parties were organised under Lieut BURNETT - one to proceed along either	

Army Form C. 2118.

WAR DIARY
or
~~INTELLIGENCE SUMMARY.~~
(Erase heading not required.)

Instructions regarding War Diaries and Intelligence Summaries are contained in F. S. Regs., Part II. and the Staff Manual respectively. Title pages will be prepared in manuscript.

Place	Date	Hour	Summary of Events and Information	Remarks and references to Appendices
			side of the hostile trench and bomb the enemy out. The enterprise was timed to start at 2 a.m. on the 8th instant. As soon as the first party tried to reach the hostile position, the enemy opened heavy machine gun fire and threw bombs vigorously. The enterprise was unsuccessful.	
	11/8/16		The battalion remained in the front line trenches until 11th instant when relieved by 10th K.N.Lanc. Regt. The trenches were considerably shelled. On relief, the battalion proceeded to occupy support trenches in MAMETZ WOOD.	
	13/8/16		The battalion was relieved by 10th Lincoln Regt. and proceeded to reserve area in BECOURT WOOD.	
	14/8/16		The battalion marched to BRESLE and next day, 15 inst, continued to march to BEHENCOURT.	
	15/8/16		The battalion entrained at FRECHENCOURT for LONG PRÉ	
	29/8/16		The battalion entrained for BAILLEUL	

Army Form C. 2118.

WAR DIARY
or
INTELLIGENCE SUMMARY.
(Erase heading not required.)

Instructions regarding War Diaries and Intelligence Summaries are contained in F. S. Regs., Part II. and the Staff Manual respectively. Title pages will be prepared in manuscript.

Place	Date	Hour	Summary of Events and Information	Remarks and references to Appendices
	24/3/16		The Battalion entrained at LA GORGUE for DIVION and then marched to BRUAY.	
	25/3/16		The battalion commenced it march to the trenches halting for the night at MAZINGARBE.	
	26/3/16		March continued to the trenches, relieving 9th Royal Enniskilling Fus in the front line in the 14 BIS sector	
	29/3/16		Battalion was relieved by the 11th Royal Warwick Regt and proceeded to the SUPPORT LINE. The enemy fired two shells on to the support line killing CAPT. D.D. MacLEAN and 16177 P¢ MOORFIELD.	

112th Brigade.
37th Division.

1/8th BATTALION

EAST LANCASHIRE REGIMENT

SEPTEMBER 1916:

ORDERLY ROOM.
No. 1071a
Date 30-9-16
8th Bn EAST LANCS. REGT.

To Headquarters
    112 Infantry Brigade

Confidential

War Diary
    of
8th (S) Bn East Lancashire Regt.
From 1-9-16   to 30-9-16.
Volume 14.

T. Mackay
                LT. COLONEL
COMMANDING 8th BATTN. EAST LANCS.

Army Form C. 2118

WAR DIARY
or
INTELLIGENCE SUMMARY
(Erase heading not required.)

Vol 14

Instructions regarding War Diaries and Intelligence Summaries are contained in F.S. Regs., Part II. and the Staff Manual respectively. Title Pages will be prepared in manuscript.

Place	Date	Hour	Summary of Events and Information	Remarks and references to Appendices
September	1.9.16		Battalion relieved by 10th R Welsh Fus and marched to Noeux les Mines and rested for the night in Huts.	
	2.9.16		Battalion continued its march to DIEVAL arriving in Billet about 12.45 p.m.	
	5.9.16		Battalion inspected by the Divisional General Major General Bainbridge K.C.V.O. C.B. C.M.G. D.S.O.	
	6.9.16		Battalion continued training in Bombing etc.	
DIEVAL	18.9.16		Battalion marched from DIEVAL to FOSSE 10 and rested the night in Billets.	
FOSSE 10	19.9.16		Battalion proceeded to ANGRES II Section relieving the 2nd Batt. R.M.L.I. Station very quiet. Our trench Mortars and Stokes fired about 20 rounds no retaliation from the Enemy. Patrols out had nothing to Report.	
	20.9.16		Enemy artillery very quiet. Enemy trench mortars fired occasionally during the Evening. Our trench Mortars and Stokes Guns retaliated effectively. Fired several salvoes of Rifle grenade without retaliation. Officers Patrol met no working parties or hostile patrols. Our Officers Observers and Snipers failed to detect any movement in Enemies Lines	

8 £ 2an

141.X
3 shub
443.

WAR DIARY or INTELLIGENCE SUMMARY

Army Form C. 2118

Place	Date	Hour	Summary of Events and Information	Remarks and references to Appendices
ANGRES I.	21.9.16		Enemy has been inactive. Our Stokes Mortars bombarded enemy front and support lines. An Officers patrol under reconnoitred an enemy sap. The sap extended about 10 yards in front of the enemy wire. Talking was heard from its occupants and several random shots were fired by them. An Officers patrol reconnoitred "Thompsons" & "Cotes" was found to be very strong round it. An enemy wiring party was driven in by our Lewis Gunners.	
"	22.9.16		We fired several volleys of Rifle Grenades into enemy Trenches and renewed retaliation. Our Trench Mortar Batteries were very active and considerable damage was done to Enemy Trenches. Also alarming a hostile machine gun firing at our aircraft. Patrols reported enemy very quiet.	
"	23.9.16		Enemy very quiet, our T.M. Battery and Stokes mortars fairly active. Patrols out nothing to report. No enemy patrols met.	
"	24.9.16		Enemy very quiet and nothing to report. Patrols out met no enemy patrols or working parties.	
"	25.9.16		Enemy very quiet. Battalion relieved by 11th R. Warwick Regt. Relief commenced 8.0 am and completed about Noon. A + D Companies from front line marched to FOSSE 10 and B + C Coys marched to BULLY GRENAY.	
	26.9.16		Battalion at rest or being instructed in Bombing etc.	

A.D.S.S./Forms/C. 2118.

112th Brigade
37th Division.

1/8th BATTALION

EAST LANCASHIRE REGIMENT

OCTOBER 1 9 1 6 :

Confidential

War Diary

of

8th S. Bn. East Lancashire Regt.

From 1-10-16 to 31-10-16

Volume 15.

W. D. Webb-Bowen
LT-COLONEL,
COMMANDING 8th BATTN. EAST LANCS REGT.

WAR DIARY or INTELLIGENCE SUMMARY

Army Form C. 2118

"VOL 15"

L.A.
15 X.
6 sheet

Place	Date	Hour	Summary of Events and Information	Remarks and references to Appendices
Foose 10.	1-10-16		The Battalion relieved the 11th Bn R Warwick Regt in ANGRES II Section. Situation quiet during the early part of the evening. Our Howitzers and 18 pdrs were firing on the enemy back areas at intervals during the afternoon and evening. About 8.0 pm the enemy threw two bombs into BULLY CRATER. About 7.30 pm enemy sent up four green rockets which split into two; no action was observed to follow.	
	2-10-16		Enemy very quiet, no enemy artillery fire to report; our 18 pdrs fired a few rounds into the enemy's back areas at various intervals during the last 24 hours. Our Trench Mortars and Stokes guns bombarded the enemy front line. The enemy retaliated with about 7 minnewerfer shells. A direct hit was obtained on Left Coy Signal Office. A deal of damage was done to front line but no casualties. Patrol under 2/Lt Taylor reconnoitred the ground in front of enemys line no enemy movement was reported.	

Army Form C. 2118.

WAR DIARY
or
INTELLIGENCE SUMMARY.
(Erase heading not required.)

Instructions regarding War Diaries and Intelligence Summaries are contained in F. S. Regs., Part II. and the Staff Manual respectively. Title pages will be prepared in manuscript.

Place	Date	Hour	Summary of Events and Information	Remarks and references to Appendices
ANGRES II	3-10-16		Owing to bad weather conditions observation in & behind the enemy lines has been difficult. About 6 p.m. one green and two red lights went up from enemy support line opposite BULLY ALLEY. No action was observed to follow. An Officer's patrol went out from Trench 47 remaining for two hours during which time the enemy sent up one very light. No sounds of the enemy were heard and no hostile patrols were out. The enemy Trench Mortars have been very active during the day. Three direct hits on our front line in Trench 52. Our Trench Mortars have retaliated very effectively, no damage otherwise. Our Trench Mortars have retaliated very effectively on enemy front & support trenches. We fired 7 volleys of Newton Pippins into enemy front trench opposite only 22.	
ANGRES II	4-10-16		Enemy very quiet only 10 Trench mortars have been fired at us. Our Trench Mortars retaliated very effectively. Two of the enemy were seen to be buried in the air and also portions of his parapet. Patrols were out one came within 10 yards of an enemy sentry in THOMPSON'S CRATER three hand grenades were thrown at him	W.B.

WAR DIARY
or
INTELLIGENCE SUMMARY.

(Erase heading not required.)

Army Form C. 2118.

Place	Date	Hour	Summary of Events and Information	Remarks and references to Appendices
ANGRES II	4.10.16		Very lights were sent up from other parts of brales but no shots were fired from where sentry had been seen. Heavy rain has caused the front line and PYRENEES TRENCH to fall in in several places. Enemy's Trench Mortars less active during 24 hours. Rifle Grenades and aerial torpedoes have been more active but majority fell short. Our Trench Guns Trench Mortars bombarded the Enemy's Front & Support Lines at intervals during the morning without retaliation. We fired five volleys of Newton Pipping from 8 Rifle Battery and seven volleys from four rifle Battery all of which exploded on the enemy parapet & in his front trenches. Two Officers patrols were out between 12 and 2 am but nothing to report	
"	5.10.16 6.10.16			
"	7.10.16		Battalion relieved by 11th R Warwick Regt. C. Coy remained in Maroc in as carrying party to T.M. Battery B. Coy proceeded to CORON D'AIX. Headquarters A & D coys proceeded to BULLY GRENAY. where working parties were found	R

Army Form C. 2118.

WAR DIARY
or
INTELLIGENCE SUMMARY.
(Erase heading not required.)

Place	Date	Hour	Summary of Events and Information	Remarks and references to Appendices
ANGRES II	13/7/16		The Battalion relieved the 11th Bn R Warwick Regt. Enemy very quiet from muenwerfers shells fell into GUMBOOT TRENCH at 9.30 a.m. Two or Three 5.9 shells fell into our line. During the afternoon a man was observed in their third line motioning to someone in front of him.	
"	14/10/16		A man was seen observing from M.20.d.50.60. Everything was very quiet opposite left Company. There was considerable activity opposite Right Company. Line walt Muenwerfer Aerial darts and Rifle Grenades our Artillery retaliation was not effective. At 9.30 p.m. we dispersed an enemy working party by our Lewis Guns.	
	15/10/16		Between 4.0 am and 12 noon to day everything was comparatively quiet, a little anything at "stand to". Battalion was relieved by 26 Canadian Regt and proceeded to Billets at COUPIGNY.	A/S

Army Form C. 2118.

WAR DIARY
or
INTELLIGENCE SUMMARY.
(Erase heading not required.)

Instructions regarding War Diaries and Intelligence Summaries are contained in F.S. Regs., Part II. and the Staff Manual respectively. Title pages will be prepared in manuscript.

Place	Date	Hour	Summary of Events and Information	Remarks and references to Appendices
COUPIGNY	16.10.16		Battalion marched to Billets at BEUGIN.	
BEUGIN	18.10.16		Battalion proceeded to Billets at AVERDOINGT.	
AVERDOINGT	20.10.16		Battalion marched to Billets at SIBIVILLE.	
SIBIVILLE	21.10.16		Battalion continued its march to Billets in HEM and HARDINVAL	
HEM	22.10.16		Battalion rested under canvas at SARTON.	
SARTON	23.10.16		Battalion proceeded to BERTRANCOURT and rested for 2 days in huts weather very bad.	
BERTRANCOURT	25.10.16		Battalion returned to Billets at MARIEUX weather continues very bad and Wet.	Appx
MARIEUX	30.10.16		Battalion marched to Billets at DOULLENS.	

112th Brigade.
37th Division.

1/8th BATTALION

EAST LANCASHIRE REGIMENT

NOVEMBER 1916

No. 1561a.
Date 30-11-16

16.X.
5 sheets

Vol 16

37/12

To Headquarters
112 Infantry Bde

Confidential War Diary
of
8th Bn East Lancashire Regt
Volume 16.

November 1916

N. I. Webb-Bowen, Lt Colonel
COMMANDING 8th BATTN. EAST LANCS REGT

Army Form C. 2118.

WAR DIARY
or
INTELLIGENCE SUMMARY.
(Erase heading not required.)

Instructions regarding War Diaries and Intelligence Summaries are contained in F. S. Regs., Part II. and the Staff Manual respectively. Title pages will be prepared in manuscript.

Place	Date	Hour	Summary of Events and Information	Remarks and references to Appendices
DOULLENS	1-11-16		Battalion remained in Billets at DOULLENS. Training was carried out daily.	
	12-11-16		Battalion moved from DOULLENS to Huts at VAUCHELLES and remained for one night.	
	13-11-16		Battalion continued its march and proceeded to BUS.	
	14-11-16	4.0 p.m.	Battalion moved to MAILLY MAILLET arriving there about 4.0 p.m.	
	15-11-16	1.30 am	At 1.30 am Battalion proceeded to the Trenches North East of Beaumont Hamel arriving in trenches about 7.45am in a thick fog. At 8.30 am after a preliminary bombardment of MUNICH TRENCH and FRANKFORT TRENCH, the Battalion advanced from BEAUCOURT BEAUMONT TRENCH between HAGER ALLEY and CRATER LANE in two waves	

Army Form C. 2118.

WAR DIARY
or
INTELLIGENCE SUMMARY.
(Erase heading not required.)

"A" and "D" Coys leading "D" Coy on the right followed by "B" and "C" Coys. The Battalion advanced a considerable distance (about 200 yds) in the fog before the enemy knew the attack was in progress, as soon as the enemy observed the attack he opened a heavy machine gun and rifle fire. The forward wave got up to within 50 yards of MUNICH TRENCH when our full gun barrage commenced. It was owing to this barrage being about to thick fog, and the wire in front of the trench being uncut that the main attack failed. On the left a platoon under 2/Lt Ywingoff entered LAGER ALLEY and captured eleven Germans. The casualties during this attack were very severe, especially in officers, ten of whom were killed. By 10 a.m. the attack had ceased. The rest of the day was occupied in consolidating a position North of CRATER LANE along the WAGON ROAD. (BEAUMONT-HAMEL – SERRE ROAD) a strong point was also consolidated in LAGER ALLEY at about K35 a 9.5. (REFERENCE MAP 1/20000 K11 – M23.) The 5th SUPPORTING BOMBERS fell back on a line which afterwards became our front line along BEAUMONT TRENCH to CRATER LANE – CRATER LANE – Trench joining CRATER LANE and WAGON ROAD at point Q5 G 5.3.

WAR DIARY
or
INTELLIGENCE SUMMARY.
(Erase heading not required.)

Army Form C. 2118.

Place	Date	Hour	Summary of Events and Information	Remarks and references to Appendices
MONTH of ANCRE	Nov. 1916. NIGHT 15/16		Battalion consolidate position occupied previous day	
	16/17		Battalion relieved by one company of a BORDER REGT. relief complete at 6.15 am. 17th Battalion marched to MAILLY-MAILLET arriving in billets at 8 am.	
	17ᵃ	2.30 pm	Battalion marched to ENGELBELMER arriving at 3.30 pm	
	18th	7.30 am	Battalion marched to dugouts in old British front line EAST OF HAMEL from ENGELBELMER.	
		12 noon	Battalion continued its march to STATION ROAD. Battalion remained in STATION ROAD for the NIGHT.	
	19th	11 am	Battalion returned to dugouts EAST OF HAMEL	
	20th	5 pm	Battalion returned to STATION ROAD.	
	21st		Battalion remained in STATION ROAD	
	22nd	4.30 pm	Battalion relieved 11th Royal Warwickshire Regt. in the front line East of BEAUCOURT. TRENCH relief complete at 6.15 pm. There was not proper trench the line was held by a succession of outposts consisting of one Lewis gun and crew and eight - from here. In front Line System.	
	23rd			
	24/25		Battalion was relieved by 11th R. War R. and returned to STATION ROAD	

WAR DIARY
or
INTELLIGENCE SUMMARY.
(Erase heading not required.)

Army Form C. 2118.

Place	Date	Hour	Summary of Events and Information	Remarks and references to Appendices
	Nov 1916 25		Battalion still in STATION ROAD until 2.30pm when it was relieved by the 21st Bn MANCHESTER REGT. Battalion proceeded to billets in ENGLEBELMER.	
	26.		Battalion marched to billets in MAILLY MAILLET.	
	27		Battalion marched to LOUVENCOURT.	
	28th		In billets in LOUVENCOURT	
	29th		In billets in LOUVENCOURT	
	30th	9.30 am	Battalion continued its march to the training area starting from LOUVENCOURT at 9.30 am arrived at VAUC DE MAISON and billetted under canvas	

112th Brigade.
37th Division.

1/8th BATTALION

EAST LANCASHIRE REGIMENT

DECEMBER 1916:

Subject War Diary

ORDERLY ROOM.
No. 55 b
Date 31.12.16
8TH BN. EAST LANCS. REGT.

17.X
3 sheets

To Headqrs
112 Infy Bde.

Confidential

War Diary
of
8th S. Bn East Lancashire Regt.

From 1-12-16 To 31.12.16
Volume 17.

J. Marks Capt for Lt COLONEL
COMMANDING 8TH BATTN. EAST LANCS REGT

Army Form C. 2118.

WAR DIARY
or
INTELLIGENCE SUMMARY.
(Erase heading not required.)

Instructions regarding War Diaries and Intelligence Summaries are contained in F. S. Regs., Part II. and the Staff Manual respectively. Title pages will be prepared in manuscript.

Place	Date	Hour	Summary of Events and Information	Remarks and references to Appendices
VALLE MAISON	3/12/16		Battalion moved to Billets at BEAUVAL.	
"	4/12/16		Training was carried out daily	
"	15/12/16		Battalion moved to Billets in BONNIERES and BEAUVOIR 2 Companies in BONNIERES and 2 Companies and Headqts in BEAUVOIR	
"	16/12/16		Battalion marched to Billets in LINZEUX.	
	17/12/16		Battalion marched to Billets in EPS.	
	18/12/16		Battalion marched to Billets in AMES	
	19/12/16		Battalion marched to ROBECQ.	
	20/12/16		Battalion rested in ROBECQ.	

Army Form C. 2118.

WAR DIARY
or
INTELLIGENCE SUMMARY.
(Erase heading not required.)

Instructions regarding War Diaries and Intelligence Summaries are contained in F. S. Regs., Part II. and the Staff Manual respectively. Title pages will be prepared in manuscript.

Place	Date	Hour	Summary of Events and Information	Remarks and references to Appendices
ROBECQ	21/12/16		Battalion marched to ESSARS.	
	22/12/16		Battalion marched to Billets in KINGS ROAD.	
	23/12/16		Battalion relieved 1st Bn R WEST KENT Regt. in FESTUBERT Left SUB SECTOR.	
	24/12/16 to 28/12/16		During tour in the Trenches Enemy moderately quiet slight Minenwerfer activity Casualties 2o. OR killed 1. officer wounded 9. OR wounded.	
	28/12/16 to		Battalion relieved by 11th Bn R War Regt. and proceeded to rest billets in LE TOURET.	

37/112

WAR DIARY

3rd East Lancs

January 1917

18.X.
5 sheets

Confidential.

ORDERLY ROOM.
No. 267 b
Date 31-1-17
8th Bn. EAST LANCS. REGT.

To Headqtrs.
112 Infantry Brigade

War Diary of
8th Bn East Lancashire Regt.

From 1-1-17. To 31-1-17.
Volume 18.

N. I. Webb-Bowen, COLONEL
COMMANDING 8th BATTN. EAST LANCS REGT

Army Form C. 2118.

WAR DIARY
or
INTELLIGENCE SUMMARY.
(Erase heading not required.)

Instructions regarding War Diaries and Intelligence Summaries are contained in F. S. Regs., Part II. and the Staff Manual respectively. Title pages will be prepared in manuscript.

Place	Date	Hour	Summary of Events and Information	Remarks and references to Appendices
FESTUBERT. [L]T.3.SECTION	8.1.17 3.1.17		Battalion relieved 11th Bn. R. Warwick Regt. Jany 3rd 1917. Enemy fairly quiet slight Minenwerfer activity Casualties very slight	
LE TOURET.	9.1.17		Battalion relieved by 11th Bn R. Warwick Regt.	
	10.1.17		Working parties found for Battalions in the Front Line	
Festubert Left Subsection	16.1.17		Battalion relieved the 11th Bn. R. Warwick Regt. 2.O.R. while patrolling between Islands were Missing and believed to have been taken prisoner over have been of Eastern and Moate from towards the German Line during the remainder of the time in the trenches fairly quiet slight Minenwerfer activity in reply to our bombardment with French Mortars Etc.	
LE TOURET.	21.1.17		Battalion relieved by 11th Bn R. Warwick Regt. and	[only]

Army Form C. 2118.

WAR DIARY
or
INTELLIGENCE SUMMARY.
(Erase heading not required.)

Instructions regarding War Diaries and Intelligence Summaries are contained in F.S. Regs., Part II. and the Staff Manual respectively. Title pages will be prepared in manuscript.

Place	Date	Hour	Summary of Events and Information	Remarks and references to Appendices
LE TOURET	25.1.17		proceeded to Billets in LE TOURET. Weather very cold and frosty.	
	26.1.17		Owing to intense cold the 11th R Warwick Regt was relieved on 26.1.16. Enemy fairly active with all calibre of Shells in reply to our Bombardment. our casualties slight.	
LE TOURET	28.1.17		Battalion relieved by 8th Bn Somerset. L.I. and proceeded to Billets in LE TOURET.	
LE TOURET	29.1.19		Battalion relieved by 4th Bn Middlesex Regt and proceeded to Billets in LOCON AREA	

ORDERLY ROOM.
No. 526 b
Date 28 2 17
8TH BN. EAST LANCS. REGT.

To Headqrs.
112 Infy Bde

Confidential

War Diary

of

8th S. Bn East Lancashire Regt

From 1-2-17 to 28-2-17

Volume 19.

W. J. Nott Bower
Lt Colonel
Commanding 8th Battn. East Lancs Regt

WAR DIARY
or
INTELLIGENCE SUMMARY.
(Erase heading not required.)

Army Form C. 2118.

8th Kings Regt

Vol 19

Place	Date	Hour	Summary of Events and Information	Remarks and references to Appendices
LOCON.	14.2.17		Battalion was inspected by Divisional Commander who was greatly impressed by the steadiness on parade, Bearing, cleanliness and fitting of Equipment and general turnout of Regimental Transport.	
	10.2.17		Battalion marched from LOCON to LES BREBIS and rested the night in Billets	
LOOS. (Right)	11.2.17		Battalion relieved the 7th Bn Norfolk Regt in LOOS. Right Sector. "C" & "B" Companies in Front Line and A & D in Support. Day quiet, between 6 & 7 pm enemy opened a heavy bombardment of Front line trenches with all calibres of Shells and Trench Mortars. Casualties 10 O.R. killed and 14 wounded. Our Artillery retaliated on Enemy front support line.	
	12.2.17		Enemy quiet during day but bombarded heavily again at night, our Artillery replied effectively. Galubs our had nothing to report. About midnight Enemy again bombarded our front line on bombardies 2/Lt Etheridge and 7 O.R. wounded	
	13.2.17		Enemy quiet during day but heavily bombarded our front line again at night our Artillery Replied effectively and Enemy quietened down. Casualties 6. O.R. wounded	

WAR DIARY
or
INTELLIGENCE SUMMARY.
(Erase heading not required.)

Army Form C. 2118.

Place	Date	Hour	Summary of Events and Information	Remarks and references to Appendices
Loos Left	14.2.17		A & D Companies relieved B & C Companies in Front line day fairly quiet but Artillery again shelled our front, our retaliated and enemy quietened on Bazentin. 18 OR wounded. 3 killed.	
	15.2.17		Enemy very quiet all day. Patrols out during night had nothing to report and no hostile patrols met.	
	16.2.17		Enemy quiet during day. Heavy bombardment on Right Company on Artillery retaliated only one casualty.	
Loos Right	17.2.17		Battalion relieved by 11th R. Warwick Regt. and proceeded to Billets in LES BREBIS Being Battalion in Divisional Reserve. B Company was attached to 153. Coy. R.E.	
	23.2.17		Battalion relieved the 11th Bn. R. Warwick Regt. Headqrs. moved from MAROC to ELVASTON CASTLE. Enemy quiet all day but twice during night patrols had nothing to report and no hostile patrols met. Enemy extremely nervous. The Battalion were relieved by 11th R. Warwicks. and proceeded to Battalion Brigade Reserve in MAROC. And found working parties for Brigade.	A.D.
	26.2.17			

ORDERLY ROOM.
No. 11c
Date 31-3-17
8TH BN. EAST LANCS. REGT.

To Head qtrs
    112 Infy Bde

Confidential

War Diary
    of
8th Bn East Lancashire Regt.
1-3-17   to   31-3-17

Volume 20.

J. Parker W. N. ter   MAJOR
Commanding 8th Battn. East Lancs. Regt.

WAR DIARY
or
INTELLIGENCE SUMMARY.

(Erase heading not required.)

Army Form C. 2118.

Place	Date	Hour	Summary of Events and Information	Remarks and references to Appendices
MAROC.	2.3.17		Battalion was relieved by 8th Bn Bedford Regt. and proceeded to Billets at BETHUNE. Battalion marched daily arriving at REBRUVIETTE on 9.3.17	
REBRUVIETTE	9.3.17		Battalion training daily and practising formation for the attack. Weather very wet and frost made difficult. Practice Trenches at LIENCOURT were allotted to the Battalion on different dates. Battalion remained at REBRUVIETTE until 31.3.17	

ORDERLY ROOM.
No. 261c
Date 1 - 5 - 17
8th Bn. EAST LANCS. REGT.

112/37.

To Headqtrs
   112 Infy Bde.

Confidential

War Diary of
8th Bn East Lancashire Regt
Volume 21.
1 - 4 - 17 to 30 - 4 - 17.

[signature] Lt Colonel
COMMANDING 8th BATTN. EAST LANCS REGT

WAR DIARY
INTELLIGENCE SUMMARY
(Erase heading not required.)

Army Form C. 2118.

Place	Date	Hour	Summary of Events and Information	Remarks and references to Appendices
REBRUVIETTE	4.4.17		Battalion moved to Billets in LATTRE St QUENTIN proceeding via AVESNES.	
LATTRE ST QUENTIN	5.4.17		Battalion proceeded and Billetted for the night at WANQUENTIN	
WANQUENTIN	8.4.17		Battalion proceeded to WARLUS. and Bivouaced at 8.30 am. Battalion wanted to forward dump and completed fighting equipment.	
	9.4.17.		The following operation orders were issued to all the N.C.O. Non.I.M. completed bommanding 8th E.Lan.R. General Plan of attack for VIth bombs. On "Z" day the VIth bombs with the 3rd. 12th and 15th Divisions will attack and capture the first three GERMAN lines of Trenches the 37th Division will follow up these trenches, advance and bstime MONCHY le PREUX pass through them, advance and bstime MONCHY le PREUX and consolidate a line running N.17.a.0.9 to Bwrw Road Junction O.Y.B.45.90. to O.2.a.2.0. to 1.0.Y.C.1.5. to Road Junction 1.32.C.D.4 to 1.25.C.5.8. This line will be called the GREEN LINE	S1.B.N.W.

WAR DIARY
or
INTELLIGENCE SUMMARY.
(Erase heading not required.)

Army Form C. 2118.

Place	Date	Hour	Summary of Events and Information	Remarks and references to Appendices
			General Plan of Attack for 37th Division after the Third Line of German Trench have been taken.	
			The 112th Infty Bde. will advance from their Assembly position in H.33.d. and N.3.b. in rear of the 12th Division with centre of Brigade on ARRAS — CAMBRAI Road and consolidate on line through N.12.c.9.2 — O.9.b.4.5.9.5.	
			The 111th Infantry Brigade will capture MONCHY and make good the ground EAST of MONCHY le PREUX.	
			The 63rd Infty Brigade will follow the line of Advance of the 15th Division and will make good the ground NORTH of MONCHY.	
			Detachments will be sent to hold the following points: Village of GUEMAPPE — Wood in O.8. beside High Ground in O.2. and KEELING COPSE.	
			Instructions for the Advance up to and the attack on MONCHY, le PREUX.	
			At zero — 1 hour Battalion will move from Bielcke to Equipment Dump between G.26.a.3.8. — G.20.c.8.2.	

WAR DIARY
or
INTELLIGENCE SUMMARY.
(Erase heading not required.)

Army Form C. 2118.

Place	Date	Hour	Summary of Events and Information	Remarks and references to Appendices
			Zero + 3 hours or when BLUE Line is taken move through ARRAS to Assembly Area in British Front trenches by Companies at 100 yards interval. The Area allotted to 8th Bn. E. Lan. R. is Present British Front System in NORTH of ARRAS - CAMBRAI Road between INVERNESS LANE and INDIA STREET, NORTH and SOUTH Boundaries and Front Line and INK STREET inclusive EAST and WEST Boundaries. A. Coy will occupy dug outs and trenches its Front and Second Lines B. " " Support Trench on the ~~Right~~ LEFT. C. " " " " " " RIGHT. A " and Headqtrs in INK STREET Companies must be able to Advance from Assembly trenches in Artillery formation. On Arrival in Assembly area O.C. D Coy will detail a Liaison Officer and 6 Orderlies to report to the Officer in command of the Reserve Bn of the 12th Division who is attacking the BROWN LINE. He will also make known the quickest way to our Batn Headqrs office which rejoin Battalion in FEUCHY CHAPEL Rd	

WAR DIARY or INTELLIGENCE SUMMARY

Army Form C. 2118.

Place	Date	Hour	Summary of Events and Information	Remarks and references to Appendices

(cont)
At ZERO + 6 hours 40 minutes the Battalion will move forward in rear of 12th Division in Artillery Formation.
"A" Coy on the Right keeping touch with the 6th Bedford Regt who will direct.
"B" Coy on the Left keeping direction with "A" Coy.
"C" Coy Right Support. "A" Coy Left Support.
Zero + 8 hours 30 minutes Battalion arrives at Rendezvous from FEUCHY CHAPEL to H.33.b.8.0. where we reform for the attack on the GREEN Line.
Battalion will form up for the attack on the Road as follows.
RIGHT A. Coy. from N.3.b.7.5. to H.33.d.90.15. LEFT H.33.d.90.15. to H.33.d.9.8.
Right Support, C. Coy. LEFT SUPPORT. D. Coy.
At about ZERO + 10 hours the Battalion will advance to the attack.
Scouts from the two leading companies must be sent out to cover the Advance of the Battalion
The LEFT will direct and keep in touch with the 10th Royal Fusiliers which move along the track through N.6.c. — N.6.d.
Objective
RIGHT. WINDMILL N.12.b.4.1. to O.7.a.5.4.
LEFT. O.7.a.5.4. to O.7.b.45.95. moving SOUTH of MONCHY.

11th R Fusiliers

WAR DIARY
or
INTELLIGENCE SUMMARY.
(Erase heading not required.)

Army Form C. 2118.

Place	Date	Hour	Summary of Events and Information	Remarks and references to Appendices
			On arrival at OBJECTIVE Senior Officer in Command of the LEFT will lead out a patrol to examine the WOOD in O.8. & extricate Battalion not dug in on the Objective. 10th Royal Fusiliers will dig in on the line of the ROAD from about O.1.c.15.10 to a point 100 yards NORTH of the WINDMILL. Tanks if refilled will be available to help us but the attack will not wait for them. Small Box Respirators will be worn in the alert position. ZERO + 12 hours FLARES will be lit on the GREEN LINE	

WAR DIARY or INTELLIGENCE SUMMARY

Army Form C. 2118.

Place	Date	Hour	Summary of Events and Information	Remarks and references to Appendices
	9th		Summary of Operations between 9th and 12 April 1917. Battalion marched from WARLUS to Assembly Area near PORT D'AMIENS ARRAS where fighting equipment was completed.	
		9.15 am	March continued to Old British Front Line NORTH OF CAMBRAI Road in Square N.29.	
		1.50 pm	Advanced to BLACK LINE.	
		3.0 pm	continued forward to Assembly Area WEST OF BLUE LINE in Square H.31.b	
		5.15 pm	Battalion left Assembly Area WEST OF BLUE LINE to rendezvous in road joining FEUCHY VILLAGE and FEUCHY CHAPEL in squares H.33.d and N.3.b. Advance was started in Artillery formation A. Coy RIGHT FRONT B. Coy LEFT FRONT. C. Coy RIGHT SUPPORT. D. Coy LEFT SUPPORT. until the leading Companies reached a line H.33.a.5.0. to H.33.c.5.0 when M.G. fire was opened on the Battalion by the enemy from the BROWN LINE. Companies then opened out in Echelon and continued advance by rushes from shell holes until the road in H.33.a. was gained where A + B Companies formed up in a line with "C" in Support in shell holes about 200 yards in rear. "D" Coy was in TILLOY LANE.	

WAR DIARY
or
INTELLIGENCE SUMMARY.
(Erase heading not required.)

Army Form C. 2118.

Place	Date	Hour	Summary of Events and Information	Remarks and references to Appendices
			Lt.Col. Hon. I.M. Campbell went forward and consulted with the Commanding Officer of 9th Bn Essex Regt. and it was decided to attack the BROWN LINE. The Essex were to lead and A + B Coys 8th E.Kn.R. were in support. The attack did not materialise. At 8.0 pm again it was decided to carry out a Bombing demonstration by way of the BROWN LINE. Captain F. EDMONDSON commanding A'Coy arranged his company into two Bombing groups with Lewis gunners and riflemen following in rear. The plan of attack was as follows. No.1 Bombing group was to advance up TILLOY LANE and Bomb to the RIGHT and LEFT to the FRONT LINE in the BROWN LINE. No.2 Bombing group to advance along C.T. in N.3.c.8.5. - N.4.a.4.5.75. Bomb to the LEFT get into touch with No.1. Group. Essex Regt. were to supply a third party to work up some C.T. and bomb to the RIGHT. This party did not turn up. Commanding Officer was informed half an hour after the attack was to start that this was so. The two Lewis guns were to assist. One hoisted at N.4.a.3.5.95 and the other at N.4.a.3.5.55. Their task was to keep up a continuous fire on the enemy parapet to prevent the enemy standing up and stopping Bombers. The attack was not successful battalion fell back and dug themselves in approximately the original trench taken up, in touch with 10th Royal Fusiliers on LEFT and 6th Bedfords on RIGHT. At 4.0am orders were received to fall back on our original organisation positions and prepare to move again to 12th Division after they attacked and captured the BROWN LINE at 8.15 am.	

Army Form C. 2118.

WAR DIARY
or
INTELLIGENCE SUMMARY.
(Erase heading not required.)

Place	Date	Hour	Summary of Events and Information	Remarks and references to Appendices
			The attack was postponed until 12 noon, at 1.30 pm orders were received to advance from the attack on the GREEN LINE as in original instructions but with RIGHT on CAMBRAI ROAD. Battalion advanced in Artillery formation with Scouts preceding the Front wave, A + D Coy in Front, B + C in Support. There was some delay in getting into touch with 10th Royal Fusiliers on LEFT, who were unable to get into line having met with H.S.S. + C. and N.S. a + C. the enemy opened with Artillery and M.G. fire from MONCHY LE PREUX then WEST of MONCHY - LABERGERE Road and RIGHT in direction of GUEMAPPE. Battalion advanced in extended order. Enemy could be seen digging in a line about 200 yards WEST of MONCHY LABERGERE Road. 5.30 pm the Battalion reached a line LES FOSSES FERMES to N.6.c.1.0 to N.6.c.4.7. held with M.G. fire. The Battalion was in touch with 6th Bedfords on RIGHT. Heavy fire of our own artillery was being opened on their but atany rate advanced out line to about N.12.a.6.0.15. to N.6.a.9.0. About 6.0 pm a message was sent to 0.C. 10 R.N. Fus. R. asking that his LEFT Company be moved to a position of readiness in rear of its two LEFT Coys. This was done. The request was made in view of the fact that touch was been lost from our LEFT with 10th R.F. S. R. At 7.30 pm information was received that the artillery were about to shell MONCHY and place a barrage on the MONCHY - LABERGERE Road at 8 pm for to last 30 minutes then Barrage to advance 50 yards every 2 minutes, the Battalion was asked to advance under the Barrage, Battalion advance to attack at 8.0 pm but was only able to advance 150 yards (from existing line) where further advance was impossible A53A Wt.W4973/M657.750,000. 8/16. D.D. & L. Ltd. Forms/C.2118/13.	

Army Form C. 2118.

WAR DIARY
or
INTELLIGENCE SUMMARY.
(Erase heading not required.)

Place	Date	Hour	Summary of Events and Information	Remarks and references to Appendices
			with 10th Royal Fusiliers. After the advance had commenced we took and cleared the full trenches which were not connected at the Sawmill at N.13.b.95.70 and HIGH GROUND in O.B. Battn. to front N.13.b.95.70. 8 LG. Bn. R. would be in Support to 10th L.N. Lancs. Company commanders did not receive orders until 5.5 am when they had advanced with 10 L.N. Lan. R. to LINE MONCHY — LABERGERE Row with advanced parties in SUNKEN ROAD in O.B. a & c. and a few men holding a hastily dug trench about 200 yards EMS of MONCHY — LABERGERE Row. Attack was held up by M.G. fire from GUEMAPPE and HIGH GROUND SOUTH and EAST of GUEMAPPE. R.I.R. Battalion was relieved at about midnight 11 & 12th inst. up to which time the situation had not altered except that Gordons were on our LEFT. between ourselves and the 111th Infty Bde. in MONCHY. Battalion arrived in ARRAS about 2.0 pm on 12 it inst and moved in Busses at 10 pm to Billets in WANQUENTIN	

Army Form C. 2118.

WAR DIARY
or
INTELLIGENCE SUMMARY.
(Erase heading not required.)

Instructions regarding War Diaries and Intelligence Summaries are contained in F. S. Regs., Part II. and the Staff Manual respectively. Title pages will be prepared in manuscript.

Place	Date	Hour	Summary of Events and Information	Remarks and references to Appendices
ST QUENTIN			Battalion marched to BILLETS in AMBRINES and rested for two days	
	17-4-17		Battalion marched to Billets in VILLERS-SIR-SIMON and rested two days	
	19-4-17		Battalion moved to Billets in LATTRE ST QUENTIN and rested two nights	
	21-4-17		Battalion moved to ST NICHOLAS and occupied dug outs in Old BRITISH LINE.	
	23-4-17		Battalion moved up to Railway Cutting. Orders were issued to Companies to be in readiness to move at once to new positions in H.Q.a. in artillery formation. Battalion Intelligence Officer was sent to report to b.d. Bedford Regt. which was then in the above trenches. Orders were received at about 5.15am by telephone on the 23rd to move to H.Q.a. and by 6.0am on what day. The Battalion was in position in the above trenches under orders to move at any moment. Battalion H.Q. was established in EFFIE TRENCH at approx.Ref H.Q. 6.12. Companies were later warned to be ready to move to the Old German Trench System in H.11.b. and H.6.c in artillery formation by Sections	

Place	Date	Hour	Summary of Events and Information	Remarks and references to Appendices
	23.4.17	1.19 pm	Orders were received by the Battalion to move forward to Chabour and occupy HUSSAR TRENCH, with its possible objective of capturing GREENLAND HILL and of establishing itself on the RED LINE originally allotted to 63rd Infantry Brigade. The Battalion was to be guided to its new position by the Intelligence Officers who had accompanied the 6th Bedford Regt. to their position in the same system. Orders were at once given to go. and they moved off in artillery formations by sections. A heavy Barrage of H.E. and Shrapnel was put down by the enemy, but the Battalion was in position in HUSSAR TRENCH by 4.0 pm. During this movement the Adjutant Captain J.W. PARKS, M.C. was severely wounded. At 4.15 pm information was received from 112 Infy Bde H.Q. that the enemy still held GREENLAND HILL and the RED LINE and that its 112nd Infy Bde (less one Battalion) was to capture GREENLAND HILL that night. and consolidate on the RED LINE the order of Battle being 11th R WAR. R. LEFT. 6th E. Lan. R. CENTRE. 10th L.N. LAN. R. RIGHT. A.C.C. finding their own S.A. hottles. 2/Lt SPEAR commanding "C" Coy was placed in charge of heading Coy. orders were at once issued to Coys at 4.20 pm detailing the above and stating that the Battalion frontage was 200 yards and that it would form up in CHILI TRENCH – BLACK LINE by 5.45 pm C+D Coys in the front wave and A+B Coys 200 yards in rear Battalion of Chie Artillery Barrage were also given and Barrage before it lifted front wave were ordered to get close up to the Barrage before it lifted.	

WAR DIARY or INTELLIGENCE SUMMARY

Army Form C. 2118.

Place	Date	Hour	Summary of Events and Information	Remarks and references to Appendices
	23.4.17		Companies duly moved off to the Assembly Trench in the order named, passing through a fairly severe Barrage however the Assembly trenches were gained, and at 6.30 Companies moved off to the attack. The enemy put down a very heavy Barrage both in front of and in Rear of the Assembly Trench this was passed through but when within 100 yards of the GAVRELLE-ROEUX Road severe enfilade Machine Gun fire was encountered apparently from N.E. end of CHEMICAL WORKS I.13.B.6.4. and numerous casualties sustained. Two hostile aeroplanes were observing the advance from approximately half an hour but ultimately they were driven off by our Lewis gun fire. The advance was over time which had become very ditrous sweeping across the open from the RIGHT FLANK the advance of the Brigade on our RIGHT was gradually slowing down owing to this fire and ultimately the Battalion at 9.45m dug in and consolidated for the night on a line about 100 yards E. of the GAVRELLE-ROEUX Road at approximately I.9.c.9.9. Being in touch with its RIGHT and LEFT FLANK Troops. During the operations one Trench Mortar and 7 prisoners were captured.	
	24.4.17		At 6.0. Hour I.M. Campbell who had been shaken (previous whole day) was ordered by Brig Gen M'Lellan D.S.O. to proceed to BdeH.Q. and Major G.W.COURTNEY who had been sent for took over command of the Battalion. Orders were received for a general attack at 4.0 hr this day but later some was cancelled and later in the day it was ordered that it 16.3m if it was being withdrawn into Brit Reserve and that it was to be distributed as follows. LA LAN.R Right Front. BEDFORD Rgt LEFT Front and given their landing points. LA LAN.R R.WAR. R.am. E LAN R were to withdraw into Support	73

Army Form C. 2118.

WAR DIARY
or
INTELLIGENCE SUMMARY.
(Erase heading not required.)

Instructions regarding War Diaries and Intelligence Summaries are contained in F. S. Regs., Part II. and the Staff Manual respectively. Title pages will be prepared in manuscript.

Place	Date	Hour	Summary of Events and Information	Remarks and references to Appendices
	24.4.17		SUPPORT into CHILI-CADIZ Trenches the dividing line being junction with CLYDE TRENCH, and this relief was to be carried out at dusk. Guides were at once warned to 2/4th F.SPEAKS and CADIZ Trench was reconnoitred. At dusk the relief started and was reported complete at 1.15 a.m. on the 25 inst. The Battalion was in touch with the 34th Division on the RIGHT this was reported to the 112th Inf. Bde.	
	25.4.17 26.4.17		Battalion held CADIZ Trench.	
	27.4.17		Commanding Officers conference at 112th Inf. Bde who Brigade orders to attack on 28.4.17, and capture and consolidate the BLACK LINE was discussed. In pursuance of the above, orders were received by the Battalion at approximately 3-0 p.m. the 27th and 2/Lt SPEAK and CUNLIFFE was sent for by Major F.W. COURTNEY who discussed the plans fully with them. Thereupon at 4.45 pm written orders were issued to 2/Lt SPEAK and 2/Lt CUNLIFFE who had been placed in command of First and Second waves respectively giving them full details of the Barrage and the positions to be overrun by them as the RIGHT SUPPORTING BATTN. Battalion was ordered to attack in Two Waves C & D forming the First Wave and A & B the Second. After ZERO + 2 when the Barrage was to commence to creep forward Waves were ordered to conform to movements of 10 L.N. Lan. R. They were further ordered to push forward to and consolidate the enemy present front line running through L8.c.h.4 and 1.7.B.B.3. and besides this they were ordered that this role was to energetically support the L.N.LAN.R. in their attack	

WAR DIARY
or
INTELLIGENCE SUMMARY.
(Erase heading not required.)

Army Form C. 2118.

Place	Date	Hour	Summary of Events and Information	Remarks and references to Appendices
	28/4/17		Companies were in their positions by the time ordered. The movements of the boys during the attack varied considerably during the day. The first wave from Reports received reached CUBA trench and 2/Lt A.C. MARGRETT who was in charge of D Coy stated he received verbal orders from Lt SPEAK to consolidate there. He dug in and at 3.0 p.m. went along the trench to find 2/Lt SPEAK who he was unable to do and at 4.30 p.m. he sent back a message to Bn Headqtrs advising what he was. 2/Lt SPEAK went ahead and with "C" Coy and gradually worked out to his objective which he consolidated. This officer was wounded early in the day and was in the shell hole, he was however doing a trench out to him and got him back and the remainder at duty until dark when he came in and reported to Batln Headqtrs. A + B Coys moved from O.B.L. keeping the first wave in view as far as possible they also reached their objective where they dug in and consolidated. 2/Lt CUNLIFFE was unable to find any of our troops on the left and fearing that his flank might be in the air and no his RIGHT was being greatly bothered by Machine Gun fire and Snipers he consolidated the Communication trench on both sides as well.	
	29.4.17		Battalion was relieved by Argyll and Sutherland Highlanders and marched to Transport Lines at ST NICHOLAS	
	29.4.17		Battalion proceeded in Busses to AMBRINES	
	30.4.17		Battalion march out at AMBRINES	

J. Campbell M/M
O.C. 8 Northumberland R.

ORDERLY ROOM
No. 651c
Date 3-6-17
8th EAST LANCS. REGT.

Vol 22

To Headqrs
112 Infy Bde.

Confidential

War Diary
of
8th Bn East Lancashire Regt.
Volume 22.
From 1-5-17 to 1-6-17.

S. M Campbell
Lt. COLONEL
COMMANDING 8th BATTN. EAST LANCS. REGT.

Army Form C. 2118.

WAR DIARY
or
INTELLIGENCE SUMMARY.
(Erase heading not required.)

Instructions regarding War Diaries and Intelligence Summaries are contained in F. S. Regs., Part II. and the Staff Manual respectively. Title pages will be prepared in manuscript.

Place	Date	Hour	Summary of Events and Information	Remarks and references to Appendices
AMBRINES.	1-5-17		Battalion training at AMBRINES. Strength of Battalion 25 & 686 OR	
	5.5.17		2/Lt S.H. Hendy evacuated sick to England. 5. OR recruits sick strength of B.	
			24. OR. 681 OR.	
	6.5.17		10. OR Joined Battn	
	8.5.17		119. OR Joined Battn	
	10.5.17		Battalion engaged in Night Training	
	12.5.17		35. OR Joined Battn.	
	13.5.17		18. OR Joined Battn.	
	14.5.17		Battalion training. Brigade scheme of Attack.	
			Lt. S.W. H. Bentley and 2/Lt W. C. Phillips joined Battalion	
	15.5.17		9. OR Joined Battalion.	
	16.5.17		5. OR Joined Battalion	
	18.5.17		Battalion marched to MONTENESCOURT. leaving AMBRINES.	
			at 10.55am and arriving MONTENESCOURT at about 3.10 pm	

WAR DIARY
or
INTELLIGENCE SUMMARY.

Army Form C. 2118.

Place	Date	Hour	Summary of Events and Information	Remarks and references to Appendices
	19.5.17		Battalion continued march to TILLOY, and Battalion in Sectors relieving Queen Westminster Rifles in N.2.d.	51.6.N.W 51.6.S.W.
	20.5.17		Battalion proceeded to relieve the 3rd Bn London Regt in WANCOURT LINE. Battalion proceeded to FRONT LINE and relieved the 1/8 Bn Middlesex Regt. B & D Coys being in Front line	
	21.5.17		C & A Coys in SUPPORT. Situation generally quiet. Enemy aeroplanes fly low over our front line, one Lewis Gun specially detailed to fire on them. 3 Patrols sent out from Battalion. Advice received that enemy may raid and one Platoon of "A" & one Platoon of "D" by order 2/Lt PHILLIPS, C. specially detailed to follow up and deal with situation at once. 1/Bom.) BOIS DES VERTS	
	23.5.17		Battalion still holds line "D" Coy furnish covering party of 1 Officer and 30 men to protect large working party. Battalion does considerable salvaging, bringing of bombs in our Area. enemy shells this vicinity & went number of gas shells	
	24.5.17		Battalion still there Lewis, enemy shells vicinity again.	
	25/17		Battalion relieved by 1st Bedford Regt and became Battalion in Support occupying Trenches near WANCOURT VILLAGE H.Q. in Cave.	

WAR DIARY or INTELLIGENCE SUMMARY

Army Form C. 2118.

Place	Date	Hour	Summary of Events and Information	Remarks and references to Appendices
WANCOURT.	25.5.17		Total Casualties during Tour. 5 O.R. Killed 17 O.R. Wounded.	
	26.5.17		Battalion in trenches near WANCOURT Village. At 1.55 p.m. orders were received that Battn will be relieved by 10th R. Ir. R. this evening and will withdraw to the HARP near TILLOY, for 2 or 3 days to prepare for operations.	
			Battn relieved as above and took up trenches in the HARP near TILLOY.	
	27.5.17		Battn rests at TILLOY. orders received from 112th Infantry Bde that Battn will be placed under command of B.G.C. 81 Infantry Bde on 29th & at 6.0.a 29d May. Men bath at TILLOY and cleaned up — a practice formation on dummy trenches	
	28.5.17		Battn rests at TILLOY. Orders received. 29d Bn. to capture HOOK TRENCH from Block in NORTHERN to NORTHERN on Night 29/30 May. Operation Orders No.113 issued detailing method of attack and disposition to assault on night 11th Middlesex Regt on LEFT. 1st Lancashire Fusiliers on Right forming line between 1st Lan. Fus. and Battn, being line drawn EAST & WEST from junction of HILL TRENCH and GRAPE TRENCH. Right of Battn being Block in TOOL TRENCH. Battalion was to attack in two waves. 1st wave 2 lines consisting of B Coy on Right and "D" Coy on Left and 2 w W were 2 lines formed by "C" Coy. "A" Coy was reserve. Operation orders no D'2 dealing with taking over by 2 coys of portion of line held by 6th R. Bedfore Regt. to enable Battn to get into position for attack. B & D Coy in front line A & C to leave at LES FOSSES FARM until night of 29/30d	

WAR DIARY
or
INTELLIGENCE SUMMARY.
(Erase heading not required.)

Army Form C. 2118.

Instructions regarding War Diaries and Intelligence Summaries are contained in F. S. Regs., Part II. and the Staff Manual respectively. Title pages will be prepared in manuscript.

Place	Date	Hour	Summary of Events and Information	Remarks and references to Appendices
	28.5.17		Battalion moved to Line B + D Coys take over portion of line held by 6d Bedford Regt. A + C Coys and carrying party remain in Shelters at LES FOSSE FARM. Relief reported complete at 2.15 am 29th inst. Battalion now under orders of 8bd Suffolks + H.Q. established at PICK TRENCH.	
	29.5.17		2/Lt V. K. WALKER killed and buried near Battn H.Q.	
		3.0p	Commanding Officers held conference with Company Commanders re ATTACK. ZERO hour notified to Coys.	
		7.45p	H.Q. move to Battle H.Q. in SHRAPNEL TRENCH N.Q. of 16J MIDDLESEX Regt. + 1st Bn Suo established there as well.	
		9.25p	Adjt called to phone + notified by 8bd Bde. that attack was postponed. Companies notified by Runners. Battalion moved by _ back. Battalion H.Q. return to PICK TRENCH.	
	30.8.17		8bd Bde warning orders that attack will be made on night 30/31 under intense barrage. Definition of troops to be assured before.	
		1.0p	Operation orders received.	
		4.0h	Commanding Officers attend conference at Bde HQ. Coy Commanders summoned and plan fully discussed. Zero hour notified to Coys.	
		8.0h	Battn H.Q. moves to Battle H.Q. in SHRAPNEL TRENCH, with Supplies + Runners. Artillery liason officers report, O.C's 1st L.F. and 16J Middlesex Regt. also present.	
		10.30h	Battalion in position as per orders B+D Coys in New Front Line 'C' Coy in HILL TRENCH. 'A' Coy in SADDLE + NEW TAPE.	
		11.20h	Enemy open Barrage on Front line + support line + M.G. fire.	
		11.30h	Our Barrage commences.	
		12.15	O.C D + C Report by Runner that it has secured objective.	
	31.5.17	12.18a	Artillery F.O.O. at our Right Flank reports objective secured + likelihood party sent out. Report Received that (A.K. BURNETT wounded. B.C. A Coy ordered to send one officer as reinforcement to 'B' Coy. 2/Lt HEATH + TYER called upon to Battn H.Q. from LES FOSSES FARM.	

A 5434 Wt W4973/M687 750,000 8/16 D.D. & L. Ltd. Forms/C.2113/13

WAR DIARY
or
INTELLIGENCE SUMMARY.
(Erase heading not required.)

Army Form C. 2118.

Place	Date	Hour	Summary of Events and Information	Remarks and references to Appendices
	31.5.17	12.53am	Report received from Lanc. Fusiliers that Barrage requires on enemy side Hook Trench, to stop heavy M.G. Fire coming from Shell hole. Artillery liaison officer notifies.	
		12.58	Report received that "B" Coy are withdrawing from Tool Trench. "A" Coy ordered to send one platoon to reinforce "B" Coy and meet attack.	
		1-10am	Lt Bentley O.C. "D" Coy reports in person that he got in enemy Trench "A" Coy of his men but was unable to hold on his flanks were unprotected & heavy casualties. Amongst witnesses to own supports & many in large number that counter attacked from shell holes and had inflicted heavy casualties to own.	
			Commanding officer orders Lt Bentley to gather as many men as he can from C & D Coys & with "A" Coy meet attack. F.O.O. reports "B" Coy back in Tool Trench. Artillery notified.	
		1-43am	Report received Captain W.J. Forster R. "C" Coy killed.	
		2.20a	Pte Colton I.M. employee arranged with O.C 1st Lan. Fus. that Bentley makes another attack bombing down trench to right while Lanc Division should down to their right. Commanding officer ascertains goo up line and position definitely and gave orders to Lt Bentley accordingly and then telephones Brigade Major 86 infy/Bde notifying what he had done. Orders were given him to stand fast and reorganise on original front line.	

A5834 Wt. W4973/M687 730,000 8/16 D.D. & L. Ltd. Forms/C.2118/13.

WAR DIARY
or
INTELLIGENCE SUMMARY.
(Erase heading not required.)

Army Form C. 2118.

Place	Date	Hour	Summary of Events and Information	Remarks and references to Appendices
	31-5-17	5.35.	Boys advanced accordingly. 8bd Inf.Bde advises by wire that orders being carried out and that Battalion is in sufficient strength to hold line.	
		5.43.	Wire from 8bd Inf.Bde confirming orders to 'stand fast'. Batn H.Q. returns to PICK TRENCH. Boys asked to send in Casualty Returns by Noon.	
		8.30.	Reorganisation complete. "B" Coy. Road Block in TOOL TRENCH with 1 Platoon. Remainder Platoon in PICK TRENCH. D Coy two SPADE TRENCH. A + C Coy. hold NEW TRENCH with 20 men and 2 Lewis Guns. Remainder of Coys. in HILL TRENCH.	
		11-15a	Wire received from 8bd Inf.Bde saying Battn return to 37 Brum. at noon.	
		1-30p	112 Inf.Bde advised of situated Casualties 2 Officers 70. O.R.	
		5-30p	111 d Inf.Bde O.O. 121 reference relief Received and issued to Coys. Battalion Relieved by 6 Platoons of 13 d K.R.R. commencing at 10-0p. Relief complete by 12-15a. B Companies marching independently to ARRAS. "b" Coy lost its route shortage at	
	1-6-17	6-0 am.	Battalion paraded at 9-45 am and entrained for DUISANS	

Vol 23

Nat Dearing

8th East Lancs

JUNE 1917

SECRET

ORDERLY ROOM
No. 176. L.
Date 30.6.17
O.C. 8th EAST LANCS. REGT.

To Head Qtrs
112 Infy Bde.

Confidential

War Diary

of

8th Bn East Lancashire Regt

From 1-6-17 To 30-6-17

Volume 23.

Lt. COLONEL
COMMANDING 8th BATTN. EAST LANCS. REGT.

WAR DIARY
or
INTELLIGENCE SUMMARY.
(Erase heading not required.)

Army Form C. 2118.

Place	Date	Hour	Summary of Events and Information	Remarks and references to Appendices
DUISANS	1917 June 2		Coys at disposal of OCs Companies for purpose of thoroughly cleaning up, bathing, noting deficiencies etc.	
	" 4	4 pm	112th Inf Bde O.O No 115 received advising that Battalion will move to IZEL LEZ HAMEAU on 3rd inst following off at 5.39 am following 11. R. Warwick Regt. Operation Order No 115 issued accordingly.	
	June 3	5 am	Battalion paraded in following order H.Q, A Coy, B Coy Band, C Coy, D Coy & transport and marched to billets in IZEL LEZ HAMEAU, in billets by 10.30 am	
IZEL LEZ HAMEAU	" 4		40 OR joins Battalion. Battalion trains in area. 2/Lt & Q.M D.G CAMPBELL reports for duty.	
	" 5		Battalion trains in Open Warfare at GIVENCHY LE NOBLE - out all day.	
	" 6		Capt J H HUMPHREYS & 60 OR joins Battalion. Battalion trains at GIVENCHY. Lt Col CAMPBELL goes on leave, Major COURTNEY commands Battalion. Orders received to march to VALHOUN AREA on 7th inst.	
VALHOUN & LE HAMEL	" 7	1 am	Battalion parades in Column of routes in order to & occupies billets in VALHOUN & LE HAMEL. Orders received that Battalion will move on 8th inst to BONY AREA by bus & road.	

Army Form C. 2118.

WAR DIARY
or
INTELLIGENCE SUMMARY.
(Erase heading not required.)

Instructions regarding War Diaries and Intelligence Summaries are contained in F. S. Regs., Part II. and the Staff Manual respectively. Title pages will be prepared in manuscript.

Place	Date	Hour	Summary of Events and Information	Remarks and references to Appendices
DONNEBROECQ	June 7		Battalion Orders No. 117 issued. Battalion moves to DONNEBROECQ by bus & road. Arrival in billets rehats to Brigade H.Q. WANDONNE CHATEAU at 1.15 p.m. Commanding Officer with O.Gs Coys reconnoitres training area.	During this period the Battalion was training daily, special attention being paid to musketry & open warfare tactics. Night operations were undertaken & specialists received attention during period 18 - 22nd June
	" 8		2nd Lt. W. F. HEATH affirm as TOWN MAJOR of DONNEBROECQ.	
	" 9		2nd Lt. R. J. PNENNAH and 11 O.R. join Battalion.	
	" 10		H. C. LAYCOCK joins Battalion.	
	" 11		T. A. B. McGARTY, R. S. CHADDICK, H. FITZ HUGH, M. E. RILEY and H. D. REYNOLDS join Battalion with 5 O.R.	
	" 14		Capt. A. B. BELL, 2nd Lt. T. BURMAN join Battalion.	
	" 15		85 O.R. join Battalion.	
			MILITARY CROSS awarded to 2/Lt. C. L. TAYLOR, Capt. R. W. CUNLIFFE, Lt. F. SPEAR for gallantry during operations 9/13 April & 23/30 April. D.C.M awarded to Sgt. W. BAKER (No. 23898)	
	" 17		Brigade Church Parade at COYECQUE. Lt. Col. Hon. J. M. CAMPBELL returns from leave.	
	"		Brigade Sports held.	
	" 21		Presentation of ribands to Officers & men awarded same in recent operations by Army Commander at FRUGES.	

Army Form C. 2118.

WAR DIARY
or
INTELLIGENCE SUMMARY.
(Erase heading not required.)

Place	Date	Hour	Summary of Events and Information	Remarks and references to Appendices
DENNEBROECQ	June 22		Orders recd that Brigade would move to BOESEGNEM AREA on 23rd inst	
NEUFFPRE & PICQUER	23		Battalion moved from DONNEBROECQ at 2.40 am arrived at NEUFFPRE & PICQUER at 9.30 am. Orders received that Bn will move to St SYLVESTRE CAPPEL area tomorrow	
ST SYLVESTRE CAPPEL	24	4am	Battalion moved from NEUFFPRE & PICQUER	
		10.30am	Bn arrived at SYLVESTRE CAPPEL area Orders received Bn will move to LOCRE area tomorrow	
LOCRE	25	6.40am	Battalion moved from ST SYLVESTRE CAPPEL	
		2pm	Bn arrived at LOCRE area. In huts at WESTON CAMP South of SCHERPENBERG HILL Marching very hot. 65 men fell out on line of march. Accommodation Bad. Received 5 huts from Division Weather fine during day men at rest at night	
	26		Companies at Coy Commandrs disposal during morning Lines inspected by Major G.S. at 11am. Baths at LOCRE allotted to Battalion during afternoon all men told fall in on line of "Daysmarch" (postponed until tomorrow morning) by GOC Division 4 O.R. and 3 officers missing 2Lt H.E. BRADLEY, 2Lt H.T. BROWN and 2Lt A.R. CARROTHERS Walton Line	R.O.Billyse

A5834 Wt. W4973/M687. 750,000 8/16 D. D. & L. Ltd. Form/C.2118/13

Army Form C. 2118.

WAR DIARY
or
INTELLIGENCE SUMMARY.
(Erase heading not required.)

Instructions regarding War Diaries and Intelligence Summaries are contained in F. S. Regs., Part II. and the Staff Manual respectively. Title pages will be prepared in manuscript.

Place	Date	Hour	Summary of Events and Information	Remarks and references to Appendices
LOCRE	27	9am	Companies at disposal of Coy Commanders for Route March during morning. Training of Specialists	
		2pm	Recreational Training. Weather fine during day rain at night	
	28		Wet morning. 112th Bde will be inspected by Army Commander at 11 am weather cleared up later. Orders received that 118th Bde will move up to-morrow and is in reserve. G.O. and Coy Commanders reconnoitre new quarters in afternoon approximately the original support line not now to later N22 d 7.0 1370 R 7 R1/60. Heavy thunderstorm in evening.	
N23 a.7.0.	29.	11am	Battalion move off to new quarters arrived at 12.30pm G.O. with 7.O. made reconnaissance of forward area during afternoon. Coy Commanders did the same during evening Aircraft active quiet during day. Heavy bombardment at 11pm. L/Officers arms Pte Ryan & Pte Richmond put on F.M.Janero. Weather fine	
	30		Raining. Coys at Coy Commanders disposal during day Working party of 250 at Eng Dump for tools.	He Phillipi

A8634 Wt. W4973/M657 750,000 8/16 D. D. & L. Ltd. Forms/C.2118/13

WAR DIARY
INTELLIGENCE SUMMARY

Place	Date	Hour	Summary of Events and Information	Remarks and references to Appendices
N22.c79	30		Mr Ryan Richmond granted 4 days special leave to France. Kit. Working party cancelled. Orders received that Battalion will move back to Dannoutre on Tomorrow.	

J. Campbell McLaren

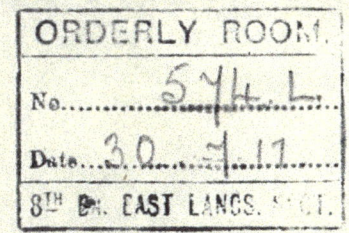

To Head qtr.
112 Infy. Bde.

Confidential

War Diary

of

8' Bn East Lancashire Regt.
Volume 24.
From July 1st to July 30th.

1917

G.W Cowley
MAJOR.
COMMANDING 8th BATTN. EAST LANCS REGT.

Army Form C. 2118.

WAR DIARY
or
INTELLIGENCE SUMMARY.
(Erase heading not required.)

Instructions regarding War Diaries and Intelligence Summaries are contained in F.S. Regs., Part II. and the Staff Manual respectively. Title pages will be prepared in manuscript.

No J 24

Place	Date	Hour	Summary of Events and Information	Remarks and references to Appendices
DRANOUTRE	JULY 1st	6.30	1st Lieut. Van Suren? Heath all leave for course	
		9.30	Battalion move to Dranoutre Area camped in WAKEFIELD HUTS. On Fri sorting party for tonight 225 along A.B. + 6 buses. Weather fine.	
	2nd		Batts moved to Battalion. On fine working party for tonight 300 firing. Recreational training during afternoon.	
	3rd		Companies at Coy Commanders disposal during morning. A Company sent 25 men with one officer 7.15 am on attachment with R.E.s Cricket match with officers of 4th Battalion during afternoon. Lt Col Campbell returned from France.	
	4th		Companies at Coy Commanders disposal during afternoon. Salvage party in afternoon. Revolver practice for officers. Slight rain.	
	5th	4 am	C.O. visited forward area. Court Martial held in Camp. Companies at Coy Commanders disposal for morning. Lt Col Kearnot returned from leave.	

A 5834 Wt. W.4973/M687 750,000 8/16 D.D & L. Ltd Forms/C.2118/13

WAR DIARY or INTELLIGENCE SUMMARY

Army Form C. 2118.

(Erase heading not required)

Instructions regarding War Diaries and Intelligence Summaries are contained in F.S. Regs., Part II. and the Staff Manual respectively. Title pages will be prepared in manuscript.

Place	Date	Hour	Summary of Events and Information	Remarks and references to Appendices
DRANOUTRE	July 5	2pm	Salvage party of 60 strong sent in afternoon.	
		3pm	Recruits met with officers & Warwicks. 2/Lt. Ryan Richmond returned from leave.	
"	6	9am	Coys at Company Commanders disposal. B & D Coys on Range. Major Crosland returned from leave. 2/Lt. Speir sent on leave. Walker line. Ramparts notice.	
"	7	9am	Coys at Company Commanders disposal. "C" Coy on Range. Visual training, judging distance & range finding. 1st Battalion Sports Day. Walker line.	
"	8		Heavy storm during night 7-8/8th. Heavy storm during morning breaking during C.I.E. parade in camp. Camp valleys affected.	
"	9	11.15a	Coys at Company Commanders disposal or Tactical Schemes. Baths allotted to Battalion. Boxing in the evening in Camp. Walker line.	
"	10	—	Orders received that Battalion will move up to N.25.d.1.1 Kemmel Hill Tramps and ... of ... Coys at Company ...	N.C.P.

Army Form C. 2118.

WAR DIARY
or
INTELLIGENCE SUMMARY.
(Erase heading not required.)

Instructions regarding War Diaries and Intelligence Summaries are contained in F. S. Regs. Part II. and the Staff Manual respectively. Title pages will be prepared in manuscript.

Place	Date	Hour	Summary of Events and Information	Remarks and references to Appendices
DRANOUTRE	JULY 10		Commander disposal of yesterdays programme & Salvage Parties. Weather fine.	
KEMMEL	11		Companies cleaning up all day. Battalion moves off Kem area at 7.35 p.m. arrive 8.30 p.m. 13 R.F. relive us at WAKEFIELD HUTS. 11.15 a.m. Brigade in support. Weather good.	
"	12	9 am	Commanding Officer received orders to proceed to England, Major COURTNEY takes Command in absence. Mr Heische Adjutant (2/Lt Taylor) proceeded on leave 2 Working parties B.100 D.100 Salvage parties of 20 from C.	
"	13.		Working parties as yesterday from B & C. 2 Salvage parties of 50 & 20 from D. 2/Lt REYNOLDS returned to duty from C.C.S. Bn Hdqrs visit forward area during day. Weather fine.	
"	14		Coys as Company Commanders disposal. D Coy carry on with Salvage as yesterday. 2 Working parties for tonight B. 50 C. 50 C.O. visited forward area with Capt BENTLEY at 4 am this morning. Weather still showery.	

NCP

Army Form C. 2118.

WAR DIARY
or
INTELLIGENCE SUMMARY.
(Erase heading not required.)

Place	Date	Hour	Summary of Events and Information	Remarks and references to Appendices
KEMMEL	July 15	9 a.m.	B.C. Coy Commanders visit forward area, also 2/Lt PHENNAH Y 2/Lt MATHIESON. Coys on Working Parties & D Coy on Fatigue. A Coy return from R.E. detachment. Weather fine.	
"	16	6 a.m. 5p— 6p— 7p—	A, B, C Coys working parties. D Coy on Fatigue. Lectures in Camp on Sanitation to D.N.C.Os. One of our Observation Balloons brought down by aeroplane. Capt. CUNLIFFE M.C. reports back from O.C. Detachment. I.G.C. School. 2/Lt LAYCOCK relieves him. Weather good.	
"	17		Orders received that Bn will move up into the line tomorrow afterwards cancelled. B.O. relays voices new Bn area in the line at 10 a.m. Weather fine.	
"	18		Working Parties and Warning Orders that Bn will move into the line tomorrow. Weather showery.	

K@P

WAR DIARY
or
INTELLIGENCE SUMMARY.
(Erase heading not required.)

Army Form C. 2118.

Place	Date July	Hour	Summary of Events and Information	Remarks and references to Appendices
KEMMEL & TRENCHES	19		Operation orders received. Bn will relieve 8th Somersets in the line. Coys Bathing. Cleaning up.	
"	20	8pm	Bn leaves camp. 4th Mx to relieve us. arrived Pick House at 9.45 p.m.	
		2.10am	Relief Complete D Coy in front line, Half Coys A Coy in F.2	
			YORK TRENCH	
		6am	C.O. made tour of Companies with Intelligence Officer. Bedfords on our right Warwicks on our left. Little Shelling. Weather fine. Casualties 4 from N.L.	
"	21	5.45	C.O. round the line. Shelling more active. Notes on new type of Gas shell being used by the Bosche. Brigadier visits Halvert to be carried out E Coy allotted the task. Ration lists daily D Coy send out reconnoitring patrol. Casualties 1 from O.R.	
"	22	11pm	C.O. visits Companies. Enemy Balloons up. Intelligence Report that enemy appear to be digging new line nr BEEK FARM. Working party of 100 O.R. for tonight. Shelling fairly active during day. Review at night, Bn HQ received marked attention. Casualties 2 from N.L.	

W.O.P.

WAR DIARY or INTELLIGENCE SUMMARY

Army Form C. 2118.

Place	Date	Hour	Summary of Events and Information	Remarks and references to Appendices
TRENCHES	July 23	6.30 am to 11 am	Act. Adj. visited Coys in the line. C.O. visited him, also went up to O.R. in evening. Intermittent shelling during day. Enemy Balloons up. Aeroplanes active all four machines brought down in front line at 8 pm. Bty fire observed S. of HOUTHEM. N. of MESSINES. Bn. has men at barricade in front of entrance. Working carrying parties of 100 O.R. for High Salvage party under 2/Lt CHADDOCK. Casualties from 7 O.R.	
	24	5 am 7 am	C.O. Intelligence Officer and First Support Reserve lines. Enemy plane turned overhead very low fire brought one of own machines down at 10.30 am in ridge line. Shelling fairly heavy, two shells used. A/D Coy accids knock their Coy HQ. No Balloons up. Carrying party from ULSTER DUMP helped fill Sinis. Working party on YORK TRENCH. Machine Guns firing from vicinity of BEEK FARM. Adjutant 2/Lt TAYLOR 2/Lt FLEISCHER reports back to Transport	W.O.P.

WAR DIARY
or
INTELLIGENCE SUMMARY.
(Erase heading not required.)

Army Form C. 2118.

Place	Date	Hour	Summary of Events and Information	Remarks and references to Appendices
TRENCHES	24		2nd Lieuts Kerr Lewis, Walker & Price from 73rd Fleischer reced from H.Q. with Rations. Casualties NIL to date. 5 O.R.	
"	25		Bn relvd by Natives knights to 8th Somersets. Work and Lancs with later on Batta.	
		5.45 am	Intelligence Officer visited all Coys.	
			Working parties from R.B. & Cois 8th left behind after relief. Taken out after completion of task. Intermittent shelling during day. Heavy at times. Rain during morning, fine later. Casualties up to noon. 4 O.R.	
TRENCHES & LANCASHIRE VILLAGE	26	3.10 am	Relief Complete. Bn more to support in LANCASHIRE VILLAGE. Commanding Officer arrived in new area from line.	
		5 am		
		8 "	Bn received orders to move back to WAKEFIELD HUTS tonight.	
		9 -	Capt Cunliffe M.C. 3/6 Sherwoods proceeded on leave. Casualties NIL.	
		4 pm	Commanding Officer went to conference with 111th Bde.	

W.R.P.

WAR DIARY or INTELLIGENCE SUMMARY

Army Form C. 2118.

Place	Date	Hour	Summary of Events and Information	Remarks and references to Appendices
LANCASHIRE VILLAGE & DRANOUTRE	26.	4 pm	Battalion moved to WAKEFIELD HUTS relieve 13th Royal Fusiliers tat same entering parties of 100 O.R. who will follow on later. Weather fine.	
DRANOUTRE	27		Cmdrs cleaning up. Kit inspection. Working parties for tonight 240 O.R. from all Companies. Busses arrived Camp. Weather fine.	
"	28		At LOBB Yet BURNER returned from Course. Working parties for A.B. & Cmdrs tonight arrangements as yesterday. Weather fine.	
"	29.	5 am	Salvage party of 150 O.R. out. Operation orders received that the Bn will move into the line again tomorrow, and places at the disposal of 63rd Bde in conjunction with 2 others. Lts RILEY & Lt RYAN left for Course. Weather wet.	
"	30		Companies cleaning up & bathing. Lt Pocock & new camp. Company Commanders visit forward area	

W.O.P.

Vol 25

War Diary
8th East Lancs
Aug 1917

WAR DIARY
or
INTELLIGENCE SUMMARY.

Army Form C. 2118.

Place	Date	Hour	Summary of Events and Information	Remarks and references to Appendices
	30-7-17	4.30 p.m.	In accordance with 63rd Inf. Bde O.O No 147 dated 24-7-17, the Battalion left WAKEFIELD HUTS, DRANOUTRE at 4.30 p.m. 30-7-17 and marched to LANCASHIRE VILLAGE (E. of KEMMEL) where a halt was made for a hot meal and for the distribution of extra ammunition, supplies etc. and finally arrived at its assembly position, as Brigade Reserve to the 63rd Inf. Bde at NORTH of GUN FARM, "A" & "D" Companies in the Reserve line NORTH of GUN FARM, "B" Companies in the RIDGE DEFENCES and Battalion Headquarters at TORREKEN FARM. Zero hour was at 3.50 a.m. 31st inst.	
	31-7-17	12.15 a.m.		
		12.15 a.m.		
		3.15 a.m.		
		9.15 a.m.	At 9.15 a.m. the Commanding Officer was called to the telephone by the Brigadier General and was asked to send an Officer to Brigade Headquarters (DERRY HOUSE) 2/Lt. PHILLIPS, N.C (Int. Officer) went over and returned with orders that "C" Company was to move up to the VERHAEGE-RAILWAY SIDING LINE via MANCHESTER TRENCH at once, coming under the orders of O.C. 4th MIDDLESEX REGT. "B" Company were to stand by to move at a moments notice.	
		12.45 p.m.	The Commanding Officer was ordered to proceed to Brigade Headquarters, where he received orders to move up "B" Company, who would also come under the orders of O.C. 4th MIDDLESEX. He personally gave O.C "B" Company (Capt. BELL AB) these orders who	
		1.15 p.m.	moved off at 1.15 p.m.	
		1.55 p.m.	The Commanding Officer received orders by telephone to move up the two remaining Companies "A" & "D" and to re-establish Battalion Headquarters at FORESTER'S POST (O.21.d.60.65) the Battalion Headquarters of the 4th MIDDLESEX REGT, where he would receive further orders. He gave verbal orders to O.C "A" & "D" Coys (2/Lt REYNOLDS & Capt BENTLEY) to this effect, telling them that further orders would be issued to them as they found Battalion Headquarters.	

WAR DIARY
or
INTELLIGENCE SUMMARY.
(Erase heading not required.)

Army Form C. 2118.

Place	Date	Hour	Summary of Events and Information	Remarks and references to Appendices
	31-7-17	2.15 p.m	At about 2.15 p.m the Commanding Officer left TORREKEN and arrived at FORESTERS' POST about 3 p.m.	
		3 p.m	On arrival, he was informed by O.C 4th MIDDLESEX REGT. (LT.COL. BRIDGEMAN) that three of his Companies could not be found, and that he had only about 100 men at present in the old front line and that the "B" & "C" companies up into this line. He also said that the B.q.C. wished to establish by means of pivots, connection with the Right flank of the 56th Inf Bde and the left flank of the 8th LINCOLNSHIRE REGT, which was considerably in advance of our line and in the air. The Commanding Officer left immediately with the Intelligence Officer and met "A" & "D" Companies in MANCHESTER TRENCH and ordered "A" Company to take up a position in the old Front Line, on the Right of "B" Company and to get touch with the RESERVE COMPANY of 8th LINCOLNS on their Right. "D" Company to be in SUPPORT in the VERHAEGE LINE. The dispositions of the Battalion were then :-	

"C" Company on the LEFT } in the OLD FRONT SHELL
"B"   "   in the CENTRE } HOLE LINE.
"A"   "   on the RIGHT }
"D"   "   in SUPPORT } in VERHAEGE LINE

Army Form C. 2118.

WAR DIARY
or
INTELLIGENCE SUMMARY.
(Erase heading not required.)

3

Place	Date	Hour	Summary of Events and Information	Remarks and references to Appendices
	31-7-17		The Commanding Officer then went up to the FRONT LINE where he issued verbal orders to O.C. 'C' Company to push out patrols to establish connection with the 56th Brigade, who were reported to be in the vicinity of the FORK ROADS (O.23.b.2.4.) and to O.C. 'A' Company to do likewise with the 8th LINCOLNS, who were reported to be at JUNE FARM (O.23.C.7.6.) He was about to leave the front line when 17.00. BRIDGEMAN arrived with written orders to cancel previous orders and to push out strong reconnoitring patrols (the strength of a Platoon) in extended order along the whole front to discover the strength and locality of the enemy's positions on our front. This was about 5 p.m. Both Lt Colonel BRIDGEMAN and the Commanding Officer agreed that this last order would entail very heavy casualties – the enemy were shelling our immediate front very heavily at the time and he suggested that they should communicate by telephone to Brigade Headquarters with reference to this order. On their way back they met an orderly (at about 5.45 p.m.) bearing written orders for an attack by this Battalion under an artillery barrage at 7.p.m. There not being sufficient time to organize an attack by 7.p.m. the Commanding Officer telephoned to Bde. H.Q. and for the attack put it until 8 p.m. The Commanding Officer then went back to the front line, arriving there just before 7.p.m. and met all Officers	

WAR DIARY
or
INTELLIGENCE SUMMARY.

(Erase heading not required.)

Army Form C. 2118.

4

Place	Date	Hour	Summary of Events and Information	Remarks and references to Appendices
	31.7.17	7 p.m.	He then issued verbal orders and directed that "A" "B" & "C" Companies should attack on a Battalion frontage in three waves, "C" on the LEFT, "B" in the CENTRE and "A" on the RIGHT. "C" Company to occupy the BLUE LINE with its LEFT at the FORK ROADS at 0.22.b.24. "B" Company with its CENTRE on RIFLE FARM and "A" Company with its RIGHT on JUNE and then JULY FARMS. "D" Company to move up at ZERO from the VERHAEGE LINE to the OLD FRONT SHELL HOLE LINE. The artillery barrage was to be a standing one 150 yards in front of the final objective.	
		8 p.m.	The barrage opened and the three companies went over. Within the first ten minutes four prisoners came back, captured from near MAY FARM and also about ten walking wounded. A report was received from O.C "B" Company stating that he had reached a position E. of MAY FARM, and had been held up at 8.30 a.m. by enemy M.G. in a copse S. of MAY FARM which was eventually driven out by means of L.G. fire.	
		9-9.30	Between 9-9.30 p.m. messages were received from all companies stating that the objective had been gained, and that they were digging in, but the extreme Left & Right flanks were in the air, and that touch had not yet been gained. The Commanding Officer returned to Battn. Hdqrs. owing to the forward telephone line being constantly cut but shell fire.	

WAR DIARY
or
INTELLIGENCE SUMMARY.
(Erase heading not required.)

Army Form C. 2118.

5

Place	Date	Hour	Summary of Events and Information	Remarks and references to Appendices
			On reaching Baton Hedge, he informed Lieut Hedges of these reports and suggested that D Company should move up to support the Front Line, stating that we had had heavy Casualties, and that all Companies were asking for reinforcements. On sanction for this move, he was about to ring up O.C. D Company when a report	
		11.45 am	was received stating that the Battalion had retired back to the old position.	
			As a result of a conference of Officers held afterwards it was found that C Company had reached its Objective but had lost three Officers – Captain HUMPHREYS, O.C. Company 2/Lieut. LOMER T.S. and 2/Lieut HEATH M.E. This left 2/Lieut CHADDOCK R.S. in command. Many parties of the enemy had been met with, all of whom had been driven off with rifle and Lewis Gun fire. 2/Lieut CHADDOCK hung on on the objective till had to retire about 400 yards owing to heavy enemy barrage.	
		7.4.18	Companies both reached their Objectives meeting with a considerable number of the enemy on the way, who were driven back. A Company especially met with a party of 20 enemy, who realizing that we meant to come on, ran away. Two Lewis Guns were opened on them and practically the whole party were either killed or wounded. Both these Companies also had to retire, owing to heavy enemy barrage	

Army Form C. 2118.

WAR DIARY
or
INTELLIGENCE SUMMARY.
(Erase heading not required.)

Instructions regarding War Diaries and Intelligence Summaries are contained in F.S. Regs., Part II. and the Staff Manual respectively. Title pages will be prepared in manuscript.

Place	Date	Hour	Summary of Events and Information	Remarks and references to Appendices
			During consolidation, many attempts were made to establish touch with the units on our Right & Left, but either the patrols never returned, or they were unable to establish touch.	
		About 10.45 p.m.	the Officers who were left, 2/Lt. REYNOLDS – 2/Lt. CHADDOCK and 2/Lt. BROWN, met, and decided that it would be best to retire to our old line. The reasons for this were as follows:-	
			(i) Owing to the state of the weather and ground, hardly a rifle or Lewis gun was able to fire, the barrels & mechanism being clotted with mud.	
			(ii) That touch was not established with units on our right or left	
			(iii) Two prisoners were captured, fully equipped with packs etc about 10 p.m. One who could speak English said they had just arrived in the line. The probability of the arrival of a new unit was confirmed by 2/Lt. CHADDOCK who stated that he saw by means of the enemy very lights bodies of troops gradually coming round his left flank, between him and the 56th Brigade.	
		11.30 p.m.	The Battalion was back in the old line by 11.30 p.m having retired by successive waves. Brigade was informed of this at about 12 midnight.	

WAR DIARY or INTELLIGENCE SUMMARY

Army Form C. 2118.

Place	Date	Hour	Summary of Events and Information	Remarks and references to Appendices
	1/8/17	7:30pm	At about 12.30.pm. the Battalion was ordered by means of pushing to establish a line JUNE FARM – MAY FARM – Road at O.23.a.5.3. Eight posts were established on this line with the exception of the one at MAY FARM, which was withdrawn about 100 yards, owing to the Heavy Arty Officer informing Captain BENTLEY that they were going to bombard this farm. Later on, another post was ordered to be pushed out about 100 yards E. of JUNE FARM, as the 8th LINCOLNS were reported to have a post in JULY FARM. By dawn on the 1st these posts were in position and touch had been established with 8th WELSH FUSILIERS on our left and the 8th LINCOLNS on our Right. The only other operation of importance was at 7.30 pm, 1-8-17. A patrol under 2/Lieut. CHADDOCK, R.S. went out to find if there were any Enemy Soldiers still left in RIFLE FARM, as reports had been received that some had been seen. The patrol reached a point O.23.a.80.15 and was fired on by a party of about 15 Germans, West of the farm. On their return they found and brought back a wounded MIDDLESEX Officer. The Battalion was relieved on the night 1/2nd by the 13th Rifle Brigade	

WAR DIARY
or
INTELLIGENCE SUMMARY.
(Erase heading not required.)

Army Form C. 2118.

Place	Date	Hour	Summary of Events and Information	Remarks and references to Appendices
	1.8.17		Before dawn of the 1st many parties were out in search of our wounded and all wounded men both from this Battalion and the MIDDLESEX Regt. that were able to be brought in were successfully sent down.	
			CASUALTIES	
				KILLED	WOUNDED	MISSING	
			OFFICERS	1	4	—	
			Other Ranks	17	69	11	
			Returns for nearly everyone were brought up on the night 31st/1st by the Battn. H.Q. Staff despite the condition of the ground.	
	3/8/17		The following congratulatory message received from Brigadier General R.C. MACLACHLAN, D.S.O., Commanding 112th Inf. Brigade:-	
			"I wish to put on record my appreciation of the conduct of the Battalion under your command on the evening of the 31st July. I hear the advance to the attack on RIFLE FARM was first-rate and fully up to the reputation of the old traditions of the Regiment. I am convinced that the position was gallantly gained, and could, and would have been held if the weather conditions had been different.	
			However, I understand that no rifle or Lewis Gun could be kept in action owing to mud, and, therefore, the advanced position became too dangerous to hold. It is hard luck that all the good work should have been spoilt by an unlucky change."	

Army Form C. 2118.

WAR DIARY
or
INTELLIGENCE SUMMARY.
(Erase heading not required.)

Instructions regarding War Diaries and Intelligence Summaries are contained in F. S. Regs., Part II. and the Staff Manual respectively. Title pages will be prepared in manuscript.

Place	Date	Hour	Summary of Events and Information	Remarks and references to Appendices
WAKEFIELD HUTS.	2/8/17 3/aa		Battalion in billets at WAKEFIELD HUTS resting, cleaning up & re-equipping as far as possible. Brigade Operation orders received stating 39th Division will be taking over front held by 19th Division and giving details of line.	
SWINDON CAMP	4d		Battalion moves to SWINDON CAMP & hands over WAKEFIELD HUTS to 10th YORK & LANCS	
	5/8/17		Commanding Officer & OCs coys with Intelligence Officer reconnoitre new support line etc. Orders received that Battalion will move to BUTTERFLY Camp on 6th inst.	
	6/8/17	2 pm	Battalion moves to BUTTERFLY Camp and takes over from 7th South Lancs. Orders received that Brigade will take over from 5th & 58th Brigades on night 7/8th Aug. Battalion going in on Left Support Battalion with one company in front of front line. Operation Order No 130 issued. Battalion will relieve 8th NORTH STAFFS in Support.	
	7/8/17	5 pm	Battalion moves up in accordance with orders.	
	7/8u		Relief reported complete. Battalion dispositions as follows:- D. Coy in VERHAEST LINE in ROSE WOOD under orders of C.O. 6th Bedford Regt. B. Coy in trenches in rear of GOEDZONE FM. "C" & "A" Coys in trenches running from DAMM WOOD to ST ELOI - OOSTAVERNE ROAD. Battalion HQ in DAMM STRASSE at DOME HOUSE.	
	8 9 10		Battalion in Support. Salvaging, working and general clearing up of trenches found by Coys	
	10d.		Order received that Battalion will relieve the 6th Bedford Regt in front line on night 11/12d.	
	11d		News received that Brigadier General R C MACLACHLAN DSO. commanding 112th Inf Brigade. Killed by Sniper while going round front line	

Army Form C. 2118.

WAR DIARY
or
INTELLIGENCE SUMMARY.
(Erase heading not required.)

Instructions regarding War Diaries and Intelligence Summaries are contained in F.S. Regs., Part II. and the Staff Manual respectively. Title pages will be prepared in manuscript.

Place	Date	Hour	Summary of Events and Information	Remarks and references to Appendices
	12.8.17		Commanding Officer visits all Coy's. Lieut. D. TARNTZOFF joins	
	14-8-17		O.C. C. Coy reports that 2/Lieut POWELL W. in charge of covering Party on night 13/14th moved outposts and was fired on by Machine Gun. 2 OR wounded; party got back to line but 2/Lieut POWELL W. and Orderly missing	
	15/8/17		Orders received that Brigade will be relieved by 63rd Inf Bde on night 15/16th inst. Battalion being relieved by 8th LINCOLN Regt. O.C. B Coy reports that Post No 5, missing, Corpl. Hargreaves + 4 OR. Patrol found equipment etc in front and two German bombs - assumed that post was raided and occupants taken prisoners. No suspicious sounds heard by other Posts.	
	15/16th		Battalion relieved by 8th LINCOLN Regt - relief complete at 3.30 am 2/Lieuts PHILLIPS, PRADA and RICHMOND wounded while coming out Casualties during tour : Officers wounded 3 Other Ranks killed 4 wounded 5 missing 6 Battalion moves to Camp (CHINESE WALL) in Support Area.	
	17th 18th 19th		Brigadier General A.E. IRVINE, DSO commanding 112th Inf Bde visits C.O. Battalion in Support Area 2/Lieut's HOTCHEN, F.W and LOCKHART joins 19-8-17	
	20th		Orders received. Battalion to move up to relieve 4th MIDDLESEX Regt on 21/22nd Aug. 2/Lieut G. HEWITT joins 20-8-17	

WAR DIARY or INTELLIGENCE SUMMARY

Army Form C. 2118.

Place	Date	Hour	Summary of Events and Information	Remarks and references to Appendices
	21/8/17	7 pm	Battalion moves up to relieve 4th MIDDLESEX Regt in Support Line & take up following positions A Coy trenches running from VERHAEST FM to ROSE WOOD D Coy " " GOUDEZEUVE FM B.C Coys - running from DAMM WOOD to in DE JAEGER CABT 6.K. Battn HQ in DAMM STRASSE.	
	22/8/17		Relief complete at 11.25 pm.	
	23/8/17		Battalion in positions above, doing salvaging, cleaning up trenches & supplies working parties, while in support to 6th BEDF REGT.	
	24/8/17		Battalion relieves 6th BEDF REGT in front line. Relief complete at 12 midnight 24/25th Aug.	
	25/8/17 26/8/17		Battalion in line. On night 25th/26th 2nd Lt R.L.A POCOCK in charge outposts of B Coy killed by machine gun fire while visiting posts.	
	27/8/17	4.45 am	Enemy raid on trenches of 5 & 6 by Party estimates at 50 in number repelled by Lewis Gun & rifle fire from posts. Est unable that at least twelve casualties inflicted on enemy who retired in disorder. No casualties suffered by us.	
	27/28th		Battalion relieved by 13th Rifle Brigade. Relief complete by 3.15 am Battalion taken to camp near SIEGE FARM from 13: R.B.	
	28/8/17 29/8/17 30/8/17 31/8/17		Battalion refits & cleans. Weather stormy. Party commanding officer inspects Battalion & Transport. Brigade operation order No 138 cancelled.	

G W Coultre? Lt Col R.I.F.
Comdg 8th R Lane R.I.F.

ORDERLY ROOM.
No. 1360.
Date 30.9.17
8TH BN. EAST LANCS. REGT.

To. Headqtrs
  112 Infy Bde

Confidential

War Diary

of

8th Bn East Lancashire Regt
  Volume 26

From 1-9-17 To 30-9-17

H.T.P____
COMMANDING 8th BATTN. EAST LANCS REGT.
MAJOR.

War Diary or Intelligence Summary

Army Form C. 2118.

Place	Date	Hour	Summary of Events and Information	Remarks and references to Appendices
SIEGE FARM	1.9.17		Battalion in Camp near SIEGE FARM. Coy. Comg. & 2nd Offs. recon. to area April Bank Canal in pursuance of Brigade Operation Orders.	
	2/3.9.17		Battalion moves to: — H.Q., A, B Coys to Por Caire. C, D Coys move to SPOIL BANK, TRIANGULAR BLUFF in support. O. R. K. S. W. R. and under orders 16 Bn.	
	3/4.9.17 4.9		South Lancs. Working Party completed 3.15 am. Watching party of 1/6 O R and 5 38th E.O. Coys.	
	4/5.9.17		Coys. moved up SPOIL BANK. TRIANGULAR BLUFF. No casualties. Battalion Working Party of 80 O.R. 2 Off. E. Shark form Battalion	
	5.9.17		host at Por Caire. England Operations good and Par Bn one bombs by enemy aeroplane. No casualties.	
	5/6.9.17		Brigade Operations Order No 146 received. Labourer working party, 2 Offs 80 Ors org.	
	6.9.17		Shelling by our own. Hostiles & enemy. H.Q. No mishaps. Coys. Of Bn. and Pal glanced.	
			Battalion relieved by 1/1 K.L.R. in Prawn Line 10.30 pm Labour Embarkment.	
	8/9.10.17		"B" Coy. left camp N.B. Bar express. "D" Coy. left camp in first Batch. 6.35 pm. known Bivouac Casualties light.	
	11/12		2 Wilts ages 85 prisoners. 58 R.L.G. 6 Bag. Relief complete 6.215 am.	
	10.9.17		Battalion march up to Coast man SIEGE FARM. Battalion move to Camp in VIDAIGNE and embarked 1.35 pm.	

Army Form C. 2118.

WAR DIARY
or
INTELLIGENCE SUMMARY.
(Erase heading not required.)

Instructions regarding War Diaries and Intelligence Summaries are contained in F. S. Regs., Part II. and the Staff Manual respectively. Title pages will be prepared in manuscript.

Place	Date	Hour	Summary of Events and Information	Remarks and references to Appendices
	13-9-17		On Conf: Battalion cleaned & Working part of 15 and 2 Off. Joined	
	14		Training done.	
	15		Church Parade. Attended by G.O.C. 118th Bde.	
	16.			
	17.		Bath. Coy. inspected by G.O.C. 118 Bde. Wire entanglements by C Coy. Brigade Communication 2nd Lt. Jackson joined.	
	18.		SIEGE FARM. reconnoitred.	
	19		Bn. near SIEGE FARM. reconnoitred.	
	20		Bn. then moved to Goldfish Chateau in reserve to 19th Division. Battalion from 4.30 a.m. to 8 a.m. watching the fight in reserve to 9th Division. Strength. 13 Off. 292 O.R. At 8 p.m. orders received from Brigade ref. 19th Div. having gained their objective & pushed forward in attack.	
	21.		Bn. to return to Camp at MT. VIDAIGNE, which left 8.30 pm.	
	22-9-17		With two guides they had no fire & no one to relieve 118th Brigade in line. At 4.35 am order signed that Bn. were on ridge at 5 a.m. but that argument ended about 6 a.m. & not until 1 hour afterwards ... when B Coy & C Coy took over from ... could the relief be completed & Cols. B & C & 2 Lt. Sharman to ... ambulance slightly wounded. 23rd 2 Lt. ... R.I.P. Richmond (slightly wounded) Captain HEWITT, LOCKHART. + Lt. Nowarth Casualties 15 OR Killed 34 wounded 48 Missing Capt. ... sent into during Tour, 22nd to 26.9.1917	A. Maufs Major

WAR DIARY
INTELLIGENCE SUMMARY

Army Form C. 2118.

Place	Date	Hour	Summary of Events and Information	Remarks and references to Appendices
	22/23/ 9/17		Battn in trenches ZWARTELEN MILL 60 Area.	
	23. 9.17		Battn received orders for move to TUNNEL. Move complete 6.10 pm	
	24. 9.17		Digging and wiring parties furnished.	
			Battn in TUNNEL. Companies carrying out and strengthening	
			Front + Support lines and 2 & 3 of the Battn	
	25.		Battn moved to SPOIL BANK	
	26.		Battn in SPOIL BANK. Tunnelers carrying out & out from Battn near	
			RIFLE DUMP. Tunnel complete.	
	27.		Battn relieved by 7th N. STAFFS. REGT. Marches to FERMOY FARM.	
		10pm	Battn reconnoitered move to camp near BOIS CARRE.	
	28.		Battn moved to Bde. New Farmers in Camp what it was visited by	
			Off. proph. D. Adjt. General went to Laurner in Trees.	
			closed up "DEAD DOG FARM, in reserve to 37th Division.	
	29/30th		Battn hard in Camp in reserve to 37th Division. New Bath + houses	
			used by Coys on 28th. Church parades attended on 29th.	

A.J.P. M.

Vol 27

War Diary

of

8th (Service) Battalion East Lancashire Regiment

From 1st October 1917 To 31st October 1917

VOLUME 26.

Army Form C. 2118.

WAR DIARY
or
INTELLIGENCE SUMMARY.
(Erase heading not required.)

Instructions regarding War Diaries and Intelligence Summaries are contained in F.S. Regs., Part II and the Staff Manual respectively. Title pages will be prepared in manuscript.

Place	Date	Hour	Summary of Events and Information	Remarks and references to Appendices
	1-10-17.		Battalion in Control DEAD DOG FARM. Lt. Col. Campbell returns and assumed command.	MAP. BELGIUM & FRANCE. SHEET 28.
	2-10-17		" do " " Finds working party of 2 Officers and	
	3-10-17.		1.00 O.R. Brigade O.O. 149 received. C.H.Q. keep move to 63rd Brigade. H.Q. in CANADA St. TUNNELS. A & B Coys to 11th Inf. Bde. in Div. Res. in HEDGE ST. TUNNELS. Coys to do fighting Kit.	
		12.30.a.m.	Orders recd. that A+B Coys by for orders.	
		3 p.m.	C+D move off. H.Q. remain at DEAD DOG FARM.	
		5 p.m.	A+B move off.	
	4-10-17.		H.Q. (C.O. Adjutant, I.O. and 5 runners with Coys.) move to HEDGE ST. TUNNELS and report to 11th Inf. Bde. at 9.30 a.m. Major POMFRET remains with Transport. A+B in BOOMIN COPSE and attached to 10th R.F. C+D in CANADA St. TUNNELS and attached to 10th V+L. 11th Inf. Bde. O.O. 3 received 11.15 a.m. A+B Support to 10th R.F. C+D. Wire from 11th Inf. Bde. that Bait: will be relieving 13th R.F. and 13th R.B. to-night.	

A8834 Wt.W4973/M687. 750,000. 8/16 D D & L Ltd Forms/C.2113/13.

WAR DIARY
or
INTELLIGENCE SUMMARY.

(Erase heading not required.)

Army Form C. 2118.

Place	Date	Hour	Summary of Events and Information	Remarks and references to Appendices
	5-6-17	2:20 am	Battalion relieve 13 P.F. & 13 R.B. in L/s of Jalbot for J.21.c.9.1 - J.21.a.9.8. "B" began left "A" on right. "C" & "D" in support. MARMITES in close support. Heavy shelling in close support. Heavy shelling of DUMBARTON WOOD and vicinity while Battalion marching up. Heavy bog made in BASSEVILLE BEER delaying relief. In line, Brigadier wick HQ.	
	6-10-17		S.O.S goes up on the left. All trans to. Nothing happens. Rain throughout day.	
	7-10-17		S.O.S. put up on the Bn. Divisional front. Artillery reply promptly.	
	8-10-17		Inter Company relief. "C" Company relieving "B" on the left. "D" Coy relieving "A" on the right. CAPT JARINTZOFF M.C. killed by sniper. Rations arrive at 5am. O.O. 149 received. Carrying party delayed by heavy barrage - DUMBARTON WOOD. Battalion HQ and area shelled by enemy from 1pm to 4am. Trenches very muddy owing to rain.	G.S.

Army Form C. 2118.

WAR DIARY
or
INTELLIGENCE SUMMARY.
(Erase heading not required.)

Instructions regarding War Diaries and Intelligence Summaries are contained in F. S. Regs., Part II. and the Staff Manual respectively. Title pages will be prepared in manuscript.

Place	Date	Hour	Summary of Events and Information	Remarks and references to Appendices
Conts.	8-10-17		Carrying work, repairing and cleaning up daily. Battalion received orders to take further attack on morning of 9th and to establish position L. edge of small wood at J.21.c.98.70. "D" Coy ordered to carry out operations.	
	9-10-17		Posts on L. edge of wood established at 6 A.M. Area heavily bombarded. Carrying all day. Ration party had 4 casualties.	J.21.a.98.70
		5.30pm	S.O.S. sent up on the 5th Divisional front.	
	10-10-17		Orders received that Battalion will be relieved by 4 Middlesex, and that Battalion will embus at SHRAPNEL CORNER, and proceed to FERME SHAFTM. "C" & "D" Coys. relieved but HQ & "C" Coy of the 4th Middlesex due to relieve HQ and our "A" Coy do not get up.	
	11-10-17		4 Middlesex HQs arrived 7am and Battalion HQ left, but is unable to get "A" Coy. C.O. reports to Brigade H.Q. but is unable until dusk. relieved until dusk.	

WAR DIARY or INTELLIGENCE SUMMARY

(Erase heading not required.)

Army Form C. 2118.

Place	Date	Hour	Summary of Events and Information	Remarks and references to Appendices
Cont'd	11-10-17		Battalion at FERMOY FARM. Casualties 20 killed 61 wounded 20 missing during tour.	
	12-10-17		Battalion in Camp FERMOY FARM. Bath and re-equip. O.O. 152 received from Brigade that Battalion will move to BREAKMAN CAMP. MONT NOIR. Pouring rain	
	13-10-17		Battalion moves to BREAKMAN CAMP. Reliefs complete 2.45 pm. Pouring rain. Very cold.	
	14-10-17		Battalion in Camp. Cleans up.	
	15-10-17		Battalion supplies working party 10 Officers and 50 O.R. for road making. CAPT. COLLYMORE. a/c reports to 10th L.N. Lanc. and arrived at 2 pm. Working Party attached to 2nd Anzac. Corps for Road repairing Etc. Three Officers join. 2/Lt. BRAMWELL, FAKEY, DOOKRIDGE.	
	16-10-17		Battalion receives draft of 140 O.R. Class "A" men, 169 bays, and 8 3 officers 5th Lewis Gunners in Dept. Draft posted to Companies.	

WAR DIARY
or
INTELLIGENCE SUMMARY.

(Erase heading not required.)

Army Form C. 2118.

Place	Date	Hour	Summary of Events and Information	Remarks and references to Appendices
	15-10-17		Officer inspected by G.O.C. 112 Inf. Bde. who expressed himself satisfied with them.	
INVERMAN CAMP	16-10-17		In Camp.	
	19-10-17		- do - WET. Left 6 men armed from Reinforcement Camp. IX Corps.	
			2/Lt. BYGRAVE joined and posted to "B" Company.	
	20-10-17		In Camp. Working parties of 104 men and 10 Officers arriving from YPRES.	
	21-10-17		Church Parade attended by G.O.C. 112th Inf. Bde.	
	22-10-17		In Camp. Working party of 10 Officers and 210 O.R. return from YPRES	
	23-10-17		Lt. SMITH joins and is posted to "B" Coy. Battalion reorganises and cleans up.	
	24-10-17		On Parade. Tactical Scheme for officers in the afternoon.	
	25-10-17		Brigade O.O. 154 received.	

Army Form C. 2118.

WAR DIARY
or
INTELLIGENCE SUMMARY.
(Erase heading not required)

Instructions regarding War Diaries and Intelligence Summaries are contained in F. S. Regs., Part II. and the Staff Manual respectively. Title pages will be prepared in manuscript.

Place	Date	Hour	Summary of Events and Information	Remarks and references to Appendices
	26-10-17		Battalion O.O.134 issued. Battalion moved to WAKEFIELD HUTS. Ex INKERMAN CAMP 1.30 p.m. Camp taken over from 13 K.R.R.'s.	
	27-10-17		In Camp. Draft of 108 arrivs from Brigade School, A.S.C. and A.V.C. James Galloday men transferred to Infantry. Posted to Companies after inspection by C.O.	
	28-10-17		In Camp. Church Parade.	
	29-10-17		In Camp. Training Programme 9-12.30 p.m Parade and 2-4 p.m Recreational Training	
	30-10-17		All specialists under their officers from 10.30 a.m Daily.	
	31-10-17		Battalion fighting Strength at 28-10-17. 29 off. 834 O.R. Trench Strength. 27 off. 499. O.R.	

J. M. Campbell
O.C.

WAR DIARY
or
INTELLIGENCE SUMMARY.
(Erase heading not required.)

Army Form C. 2118.

S E Lane R

VI 28

Place	Date	Hour	Summary of Events and Information	Remarks and references to Appendices
	1/4/17		Battn. in Camp, training.	
	2/4/17		Commemoration Service. (Rehearsal)	
	3/4/17		Battn. in Camp. In training 9-12.30 2-4 Recreation	
	4/4/17		Battn. attended Brigade Commemoration Service and a marched past Divl. General.	
	5/4/17		"C" Coy. represents battalion in Bde: Yukon Pack competition and comes second to Bedford. Refreshments with them. Brigade.	
	6/4/17		Warning Order received that Brigade will be relieving 56th. Inf. Bde on 8th inst. Preparing to relieving 57th on night of 9/10. 2/Lt. Owens rejoins from instructing at VI Corp. School.	
	7/4/17		In training. O.O. 155 received.	
	8/4/17		Battn. O.O. 155 issued. Battn. moves to BEGGARS REST. Left N5a6.5.5.6.10. HQTS at 10.35. arrived 1.26 p.m. Divisional Yukon pack to fatten Battn. mr. 25	
	9/4/17		Battn. O.O. 156 issued. Batty. Move to B.S.E. school. Left BEGGARS REST. 1.30 p.m.	

WAR DIARY
or
INTELLIGENCE SUMMARY.
(Erase heading not required.)

Army Form C. 2118.

Place	Date	Hour	Summary of Events and Information	Remarks and references to Appendices
	9/7/17		Relieved the 8 N. STAFFS. "E" Coy. SPOIL BANK. "B" Coy. LARCH WOOD. TUNNELS. "A" Coy. A146 TUNNELS. H.Q. A146 TUNNELS. "D" Coy. CORNER HOUSE. "C" Coy have 80 men on Working Party with 2nd CANADIAN TUNNELLING Co. at SPOIL BANK. Relief complete 3.45 p.m. Casualties 1. Killed. "D" Coy under orders of 6th BEDFR. Bats. O.O. 91 received 6.30 p.m. Four battalions to be in Front Line. Visited by Brigadier and Staff Captain.	
	10/7/17		C.O. Second in Command, Adj. I.O. reconnoitre front positions. Baths. O.O. 157 issued 10.35 p.m. Baths takes over left North Subsection. "D" Coy Lt. Bay. "A" Coy. Right. Coy. "C" Coy. A146. "B" Coy. IMPERFECT COPSE. H.Q. FUSILIER DUGOUTS.	
	11/7/17		Brigadier visits, also G.O.C. 37 Division.	
	12/7/17			

WAR DIARY
or
INTELLIGENCE SUMMARY.

(Erase heading not required.)

Army Form C. 2118.

Instructions regarding War Diaries and Intelligence Summaries are contained in F. S. Regs., Part II. and the Staff Manual respectively. Title pages will be prepared in manuscript.

Place	Date	Hour	Summary of Events and Information	Remarks and references to Appendices
	13/4/17		Battn. in line. Casualties 1 W.A.	
	14/4/17		Brigadier visits also 11th Bn. Bde. Brigadier. 20 Ploughmen to be sent home. Enter. Company Relief.	
	15/4/17		C.O. and all Coy. Officers of 13 K.R.R. come to look over. Warning Order re Relief received 9 a.m. Bde. 00158 received 2.30 pm. Relief complete 2.30 am.	
	16/4/17		2 Offs. join the line. 2/Lt. Nisbett - Dwer 6 "A" Coy. 2/Lt. Williams 6 "B" Coy. Battn. in line. Visited by Brigadier. Relieved the 13 K.R.R. in line. C.O. of 13 K.R.R. arrived by 7 pm. "A" & "D" Coys. out before Moonlight. Relief complete 6.30 am.	
	17/4/17		Battalion in REGNIER REST. Found Working Party of 100 in afternoon. Total myht.	
	18/4/17		Working Party as above. C.O. attended Council of Enquiry at WARWICKS LOSSES	
	19/4/17			

Army Form C. 2118.

WAR DIARY
or
INTELLIGENCE SUMMARY.
(Erase heading not required.)

Instructions regarding War Diaries and Intelligence Summaries are contained in F. S. Regs., Part II. and the Staff Manual respectively. Title pages will be prepared in manuscript.

Place	Date	Hour	Summary of Events and Information	Remarks and references to Appendices
	20/1/17		Working Party all day.	
	21/1/17		do	
	22/1/17		do	
	23/1/17		work.con. C.O.reconnoitres D.L.Les Camp. Brigade O.O.159 received	
			Working Parties. C.O. reconnoitres Section of line likely to be held	
	24/1/17		Batta. O.O.139 issued.	
	25/1/17		Moved to De Les Camp. Left at 2.5pm arrived at 4 o'clock.	
	26/1/17		Battn. cleans up. Working Party of 1 Off and 20 men.	
	27/1/17		Batth at Baths.	
	28/1/17		Batth. on Salvage all day.	
	29/1/17		do	
	30/1/17		Batth at Baths.	

J.N.Campbell Lt Colonel
Comdg 7/10th F LANC R

ORDERLY ROOM.
No. 242 M
Date 31-12-17
8TH BN. EAST LANCS. REGT.

To. Headqtrs
112 Infy Bde.

Confidential
War Diary
of
8th (S). Bn East Lancashire Regt.
Volume 28.
From 1/12/17 To 31/12/17

[signature] Lt. COLONEL
COMMANDING 8th BATTN. EAST LANCS REGT

Army Form C. 2118.

WAR DIARY
or
INTELLIGENCE SUMMARY.
(Erase heading not required.)

Place	Date	Hour	Summary of Events and Information	Remarks and references to Appendices
DE ZONBal	1. 12/7		Battalion at Rest. Battalion parade under Company Arrangements. Representative of 111th Inf Bde visited and reconnoitred DE ZON bank	
" "	2. 12/7		Warning Order received from 112 Inf Bde that Brigade would relieve 63rd Inf Bde on night 5/6/17. Battalion in Training under Company Arrangements. 112 Inf Bde Operation Order 159 Received.	
" "	3. 12/7		Battalion in Training under Company Arrangements. Battalion received.	
" "	4. 12/7		Entraining orders issued at 9.0 am. Battalion entrains at KILMARNOCK at 1.30 pm. Two Trains allotted Battalion arrived at SPOIL BANK at 3.30 pm Battalion relieved the 10th York Lancs Regt, in RIGHT CENTRE SUB SECTOR (ZANDVOORDE) "A" Company on the Right "B" Company were left Company in Support in RAILWAY TRENCH (J.9.d.3) "C" Coy in Support in SPOIL BANK	

WAR DIARY
or
INTELLIGENCE SUMMARY.
(Erase heading not required.)

Army Form C. 2118.

Place	Date	Hour	Summary of Events and Information	Remarks and references to Appendices
	5/12/17		Battalion Headqts went in RAILWAY TRENCH. Relief was complete at 7.15 pm. No casualties	
	6/12/17		Battalion in the line. Brigadier General IRVING D.S.O. and Brigade Major visited Battalion	
	7/12/17		Battalion in line. Working parties were working every night. No casualties	
	8/12/17		Battalion Operation Order 160 A. issued for inter relief of Battalions on night 9/10 d	
	9/12/17		Battalion in the line, at 12.5am RAILWAY GROUP heavily shelled by enemy. 2/Lt J.J. SHAW wounded, one O.R. Killed and one O.R. wounded	
	10/12/17		Enemy artillery fairly active. One O.R. Died of wounds 2 O.R. wounded	
	11/12/17		Battalion in line. 2/Lt H.J. BROWN. M.C. rejoined	
	12/12/17		Battalion in line 112 Inf. Bde. O.O. 161 received at 7.15 am C.1 after Battalion D. Order 161 issued at 8.0 pm	

WAR DIARY
or
INTELLIGENCE SUMMARY.
(Erase heading not required.)

Army Form C. 2118.

Place	Date	Hour	Summary of Events and Information	Remarks and references to Appendices
	13/12/15		Battalion in line. Enemy quiet.	
	14/12/15		Relief by 13th R.F. complete at 1.20 a.m. Battalion moved to huts at RIDGE WOOD.	
RIDGE WOOD	15/12/15		2.O.B Dinwinnie the Transport lines. Battn T.D. Lee South Lane. R. 2/Lts N.G. Bradley J.H. Deverell, R.O. Davies, G.W. Fuller R.N. Rolson and Lieut S.F. Robinson James Battalion	
"	16/12/15		Battalion Working parties of 265 men found for forward Area	
"	17/12/15		Battalion on working parties in forward Area	
"	18/12/15		Battalion on working parties in forward Area wounded on A.A defence at SPOILBANK.	
"	19/12/15		2.O.B 37th Divn and 2.O.B 112 Inf. Bde received batty.	
	20/12/15		working parties & revenue Battalion on working parties in forward Area 112 Inf Bde O.O.162. Received	(To) (5/)

WAR DIARY
or
INTELLIGENCE SUMMARY.
(Erase heading not required.)

Army Form C. 2118.

Place	Date	Hour	Summary of Events and Information	Remarks and references to Appendices
RIDGE WOOD	21/12		Battalion on working parties in forward area. Battalion Orders No. 162 issued. Battalion moved to DE ZON. Bank under command of Captain LEE. Lt Col Hon I.N. Bampfylde returned. Major H.T. Confret attended lecture at 112 Inf. Bde Headqtrs. Battalion arrived in DE ZON. Camp at 2.50 pm.	
DE ZON	22/12		Battalion found working parties in forward area. Lt Col Hon I.N. Bampfylde attended conference at 37th Divn HQ.	
	23/12		Battalion on working parties in forward area. Church Parade at Y.M.C.A SCHERPENBURG. Captain LEE, in charge of Battalion Church Parade.	
	24/12		Battalion on working parties in forward area.	
	25/12		Xmas Day. Battalion on Church Parade. A.D.C. 112 Inf. Bde attends Church Parade.	(Tobac)[?]

Army Form C. 2118.

WAR DIARY
or
INTELLIGENCE SUMMARY.
(Erase heading not required.)

Instructions regarding War Diaries and Intelligence Summaries are contained in F.S. Regs., Part II. and the Staff Manual respectively. Title pages will be prepared in manuscript.

Place	Date	Hour	Summary of Events and Information	Remarks and references to Appendices
DE ZON	26/12		Battalion found Working Parties. 2/Lt. E.B. Burke joins Battalion	
"	27/12		Battalion in Camp. Lt Col Hon J.M. Campbell attached to R.E.B. for a course. B/O O.O. 163 received	
"	28/12		Battalion parades in Camp under Company Arrangements. Battalion Operation Order 163 issued	
"	29/12		Lt.Col. Hon J.M. Campbell rejoins from R.E.C. Battalion leaves DE ZON camp at 1.40 entrains at KILMARNOCK siding for SPOIL BANK at 2.0 pm	
LINE	29/30		Battalion relieves 10th York & Lancs in RIGHT CENTRE SUBSECTOR. Relief complete 7.30 pm A Coy on right. D Coy on left. B Coy in RAILWAY TRENCH in Support. C Coy originally orders to SPOIL BANK brought up to RAILWAY TRENCH in Support.	(sgd)
			No Casualties.	
	30		IN LINE. Situation quiet all day	
	31		In Line. Situation quiet. 2. O.R. Killed 3 wd by Shell which burst in RAILWAY TRENCH.	
	31/1st	12.1am	A/4 Coy relief C relieving D on right and B relieving A on left. Relief complete 6pm Enemy artillery fires on S.O.S. lines — intense file for 2 minutes from 11.50pm to 11.52pm. No reply from Enemy.	J.M. Campbell Lt Col

Army Form C. 2118.

WAR DIARY
or
INTELLIGENCE SUMMARY.
(Erase heading not required).

Arthur St Etienne Ry
Vol 30

Place	Date	Hour	Summary of Events and Information	Remarks and references to Appendices
1-1-18	1/1/18		Battalion in line. Weather very bad. Fairly quiet day. Relief B by Relieve A by and "C" by Relieve "D" by	
	2/18		Intermittent Shelling of "Railway Trench" by Enemy. A large number of Gas Shells used. One off. Killed and 6 wounded. Gassed by direct hits on Shelters	
	3/18		Duties by Relief A relieves B on Right D Relieves "C" on Left.	
	4/18 5/18		Enemy very Quiet all day. Battalion relieved by 13th R.F. and moves to RIDGE WOOD Camp. Relief complete by 6.30 pm.	
	6/18		Battalion in Camp. Baths at Confrerie Lower allotted. Battalion Kit inspection and deficiencies noted	
	1/18		Working Party of 5. Offrs and 100. OR. supplied by C+D Coys to work in forward area. C + D Coys	

WAR DIARY
or
INTELLIGENCE SUMMARY.
(Erase heading not required.)

Army Form C. 2118.

Place	Date	Hour	Summary of Events and Information	Remarks and references to Appendices
	8/3		At Company Commanders Parade Coys work on cleaning camp and making minor repairs.	
	9/3		Coys work on cleaning camp etc. Major H.T. Pontret received orders to join 30th Division.	
	10/3		Battalion move to LA BELLE HOTESSE / BLARINGHEM area by Road + Rail. Battalion entrains at DICKEBUSCH and detrains at EBBLINGHEM at 7.35 h marched to Billets and entrains in at 10-15 h Major E.W. Hunter Gray joins as 2nd in Command.	
	11-12		Coy trains as per programme issued and Special attention being paid to Musketry + Elementary Squad + Arms Drill. Specialists train under Specialist Officer	
	13		Battalion attends Church Parade.	
	14th		Coys train in Billets owing to inclement weather	C.K. [signature]

Army Form C. 2118.

WAR DIARY
or
INTELLIGENCE SUMMARY.
(Erase heading not required.)

Instructions regarding War Diaries and Intelligence Summaries are contained in F. S. Regs., Part II. and the Staff Manual respectively. Title pages will be prepared in manuscript.

Place	Date	Hour	Summary of Events and Information	Remarks and references to Appendices
La Belle Hotesse	18/8		Battalion parade under Commanding Officer. All Blankets disinfested.	
	19/1/18		Boys, bans on tea programme. O.O.'s received re move to DICKEBUSCH.	
	20/1/18		Battalion attends Church Parade. Transport moves to new area under Brigade arrangements.	
	21/1/18		Battalion parade at 7·10a and marches to EBBLINGHEM entraining at 9·15 am arriving DICKEBUSCH at 12·30h. March to Billets in DICKEBUSCH whoding in Billets at 1·15 pm. Lt Col. Hon J.M. Campbell. D.S.O. goes to 15. C.C.S. Major G.W. Hunter Gray rejoins 63rd Brigade. Captain T.D. Lee. assumes command of Battalion.	
DICKEBUSCH	22/1/18		Working party of 6 O.H. + 215 O.R. an ammunition Officer found for Ammunition Ounces.	
	23/1/18		Working party of 6 O.H. + 275 O.R. found for forward Ounces.	
	24/1/18		Enemy shelled DICKEBUSCH until H.W. and approx. 7 rounds G.S. Lac	

A6943. Wt. W1142/M160. 350,000 12/16. D.D.&I. Forms/C/2118/14.

WAR DIARY
or
INTELLIGENCE SUMMARY.
(Erase heading not required.)

Army Form C. 2118.

Place	Date	Hour	Summary of Events and Information	Remarks and references to Appendices
	28/8		fatey in village. Working party of 6 off + 275 O.R. found One O.R. wounded.	
	29/8		Working Party of 6 off + 275 O.R. found. Party for Forward Area. Every other DICKEBUSCH on 29 with H.V. approximately 15 shells dropped into	
	30/8		Village. O.M. store hit as 2 O.R. Wounded. Major E.S. Jalopin Junior Battalion and assumed Command vice Captain T. Bryce. 6 off + 250 O.R. Working Parties found for forward area	
	31/8		" " " Orders received that Battalion will be disbanded & that 20 off & 400 O.R. will join 11th Battalion East LANCASHIRE Regt.	

Signed Major

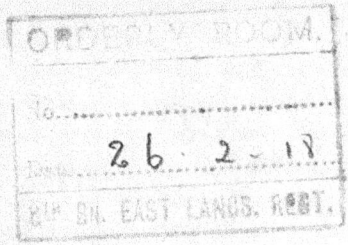

To A.G.

Confidential

War Diary

of

8 Bn East Lancashire Rgt.

From 1-2-18 To 22-2-18

Volume 31.

CAPTAIN.

Army Form C. 2118.

WAR DIARY
or
INTELLIGENCE SUMMARY.
(Erase heading not required.)

Instructions regarding War Diaries and Intelligence Summaries are contained in F. S. Regs. Part II. and the Staff Manual respectively. Title pages will be prepared in manuscript.

Place	Date	Hour	Summary of Events and Information	Remarks and references to Appendices
DICKEBUSCH	1-2-18		Nominal Roll of 20 Officers & 400 O.R. prepared for transfer to 11th Bn. E. La. R. Captain G.W. Hartley was chosen in charge with following Officers. Captain J.R. Fleming, Lieut. C.W. Pigott, Lieut. A.E. Margoth, Heuits. R. Owen, N.S. Chaddock M.C., N.C. Laycock, D.L. Arthur, E. Lyes, E.D. Turner, E.W. Hotchen, A.R. Carruthers, J.P. Richards, E. Bygrave, C.A. Craven, S. Barnaby, A. Bell, R.E. Gainess, M. Fuller, R.N. Robson.	
do	2.2.18		Battalion musters for draft and all warned by Captain Lt. Taylor, M.C. Adjutant. Orders received that remainder of Battalion will move to BANDRINGHEM on its bus and that draft to 11th Bn. E. La. R. will entrain at 8.30 am 4 a.c. for ABEELE.	
do	3/2/18		Relieving party under Lt. H.D. Reynolds M.C. moves off.	
	4/2/18.		Draft entrains at 8.28 am for ABEELE. At 12.15 Battn marched to DICKEBUSCH Station and entrains for EBBLINGHEM. Battn detrains at EBBLINGHEM and marches to BANDRINGHEM.	

Army Form C. 2118.

WAR DIARY
or
INTELLIGENCE SUMMARY.
(Erase heading not required.)

Instructions regarding War Diaries and Intelligence Summaries are contained in F. S. Regs., Part II. and the Staff Manual respectively. Title pages will be prepared in manuscript.

Place	Date	Hour	Summary of Events and Information	Remarks and references to Appendices
BANDRINGHEM	5.13		LE HUVET arrive in Billets at 6.15 to Battalion commence training at BANDRINGHEM.	
	6.13		Lt Col Hon J.M.Campbell DSO rejoins Battalion from BASE.	
do	7.18 to 12.13		During this period Battalion train. Special attention being paid to Musketry & Company Drill.	
	13.13		Orders received that Battalion will move to Reinforcement Camp at BERTHEN and await orders.	
do	14.13		Lt Col Hon J.M.Campbell DSO proceeds on Leave. Battalion marches to EBBLINGHEM and Entrains. Detrains at GODEWAERVELDE and marches to Camp. Arrive Camp at 2.15 p.	
	16.13		Training under Bgy Commander. Special attention paid to battle drill.	
	20.13		To complete me likely to be sent away on Draft.	
			Majs S.S. Judge receives orders to join 9th N. Staffs on 2nd A.	
			Orders received that Battalion will move to WIPPENHOCK with other details Regiments at and will form 15 Entrenching Battalion.	

Army Form C. 2118.

WAR DIARY
or
INTELLIGENCE SUMMARY.
(Erase heading not required.)

Instructions regarding War Diaries and Intelligence Summaries are contained in F. S. Regs., Part II. and the Staff Manual respectively. Title pages will be prepared in manuscript.

Place	Date	Hour	Summary of Events and Information	Remarks and references to Appendices
BERTHEN.	21.		Captain J T Fee. Captain E L Taylor M.C. Lt H.S. Robinson 2/Lt Broad 2/Lt Estabelle 2/Lt J.B. Hotchen 2/Lt Vincent Davies, 2/Lt H.E. Bowles, Captain H.F. Norman M.S. Hon Lt & N D/S Bamber 2/Lt T.A.B. McGratchy 2/Lt M.E. Ruley Captain E.B. Smith Captain & Supdr M.C & 2/Lt H.T.Brown M.C and R.S.M. all R.S.M's. C.Q.M.S's and Sgts on Headqtr left GODSWAERVELDE. at 11-49 a.m. and arrived at ETAPLES at 9-15 p.m. for 6 pm pending on completion of disbandment of 8 Bn East Lancashire Regt.	

www.ingramcontent.com/pod-product-compliance
Lightning Source LLC
Chambersburg PA
CBHW081525160426
43191CB00011B/1684